IMAGES
of America

BISMARCK

NORTH DAKOTA

This aerial, taken before December 1930, shows the growth of Bismarck in the early 1900s. In the background are the Capitol Building and the Liberty Memorial Building on the Capitol grounds. The Capitol housed the territorial government after it moved to Bismarck from Yankton in southern Dakota Territory. The cornerstone was laid on September 5, 1883.

The Capitol Building burned on December 28, 1930, and a "skyscraper" capitol replaced it. The Great Hall of the new Capitol connects the legislative wing and the administrative office tower. Black marble from Tennessee and Belgium and Montana Yellowstone travertine make North Dakota's statehouse distinctive. The Supreme Court wing was added in 1981. (SHSND 389–1)

The cover photo, taken in 1946, shows the intersection of 4th Street and Broadway Avenue in downtown Bismarck, and the hustle and bustle of this growing, vibrant city.

IMAGES
of America

BISMARCK

NORTH DAKOTA

Cathy A. Langemo

WritePlus Inc.

ARCADIA
PUBLISHING

Published by Arcadia Publishing
Charleston, South Carolina

Library of Congress Catalog Card Number: 2002106325

For all general information contact Arcadia Publishing at:
Telephone 843-853-2070
Fax 843-853-0044
E-mail sales@arcadiapublishing.com
For customer service and orders:
Toll-Free 1-888-313-2665

Visit us on the Internet at www.arcadiapublishing.com

POPULATION TABLE 1880–2000

YEAR	BURLEIGH COUNTY	BISMARCK
1880	3,246	1,788
1890	4,247	2,186
1900	6,081	3,319
1910	13,087	5,443
1920	15,578	7,122
1930	19,769	11,090
1940	22,736	15,496
1950	25,673	18,640
1960	34,016	27,670
1970	40,714	34,703
1980	54,811	44,485

CONTENTS

ACKNOWLEDGMENTS

Many thanks to all who assisted in the production of this book, including:

- Arcadia Publishing and Samantha Gleisten for assistance with this project;
- The State Historical Society of North Dakota for the use of its extensive and valuable photo archives, especially to Merl Paaverud and Gerald Newborg for permission to use the photos at no cost and to Sharon Silengo, photo archivist, for her advice and assistance in selecting, scanning, and recording the photos;
- Those holding other photo collections I used for the book, including Kathy and Poppy Fowler of Fowler Photography; Dave Bundy, editor, and Vicky Weiss, library assistant, at the *Bismarck Tribune*; and Rob Keller and Jonathan Haugen, in the public information office of the North Dakota Army National Guard;
- David Luyben, of David Luyben Graphics, who assisted in scanning some final photos.

They all helped to make this pictorial history of Bismarck complete.

Lastly, and most importantly, I am publicly thanking my wonderful husband, Richard "Rick" C. Knudson Jr., whose advice, willingness to be ignored for days (sometimes even weeks) at a time, and offers of financial assistance when necessary make it possible for me to be involved in very personally satisfying projects such as this one. Thanks so much, Rick!

This 1893 street scene appears to be looking east on Main Avenue. It's from a postcard that reads on the back, "Bismarck when KF left it in 1893—looking east." (SHSND 264–33)

INTRODUCTION

Before North Dakota became a state in November 1889, Bismarck had been the territorial capitol for all of Dakota Territory since 1883, when the city offered 160 acres and $100,000 to move the capitol from Yankton in southern Dakota Territory. Therefore, it was natural that Bismarck be named the capitol of the new state, and the territorial capitol building became the headquarters for North Dakota's government.

In addition to being the state's capitol, Bismarck was also named the county seat of Burleigh County, organized in July 1873 and named after Dr. Walter A. Burleigh. E.A. Williams, who had his law office at 16 North 3rd Street in 1879, served as the first president of the County Commissioners, with Clement Lounsbery as secretary. Maj. William Woods was the county's first sheriff, and Alexander McKenzie, a prominent political figure, also served as sheriff for a number of years.

Dr. Burleigh contracted with Edmond Hackett in June 1872 to construct the first buildings in Bismarck. It was a warehouse, later the site of the Merchants Hotel, and a mess room, which operated from 1872–1877 and was later the site of Justus Bragg's Montana Market at 26 Main Avenue. By 1884, the Dietrich Brothers were operating the Montana Market, then located on the southeast corner of 3rd Street and Main Avenue. One of the earliest businesses was Shaw and Cathcart store. W.B. Shaw arrived in May 1872 and set up shop on the corner of 4th Street and Main Avenue.

The town site was laid out by J.E. Turner, an engineer for the Northern Pacific Railroad (NPRR), assisted by George W. Sweet and John Bowen. Named Edwinton in February 1873 for Edwin F. Johnson, a NPRR employee, the city was renamed Bismarck in July 1873. With this gesture, the railroad leaders hoped to receive attention from Germany's "Iron Chancellor" Otto Von Bismarck to finance the railroad's continued westward expansion. Bismarck was incorporated in January 1875, and John A. McLean became the first elected mayor. He arrived in the area in 1873 and was instrumental in determining the city's location.

Linda Warfel Slaughter, the wife of Dr. B.F. "Frank" Slaughter, the post surgeon at Camp Hancock, was a notable character in the community and one of the first women in Bismarck. While stationed at Camp Hancock, established in 1872 to protect the railroad and now a state historic site, she became the postmistress of Bismarck and wrote extensively for the *Bismarck Tribune*, helping to record 1870s life in the area. As a teacher, she also started the first school in Bismarck, a private one held at the Congregational Church at 5th Street and Thayer Avenue. Her sister, Aidee Warfel, was one of the teachers. After he left the military, Dr. Slaughter set up office in the Pioneer Drug Store building.

As the nearest point of civilization to the Black Hills of southern Dakota Territory, Bismarck served as an important starting point for the military's exploration in 1874, after gold was discovered in the Black Hills. Goldseekers, with their trains of freighter wagons, left Bismarck for the 300-mile trek through Indian country to the Black Hills.

Until the railroad came through in 1873, the Bismarck area was dependent on the Missouri River for supplies, transportation, visitors, and news. Trains provided greater opportunities for traveling to and from the city, and roads and automobiles made it even more convenient.

At the beginning of the Great Depression decade, Bismarck and North Dakota lost their Capitol building. It turned out to be as much a blessing as a disaster, though, because building a new Capitol created employment opportunities for many who may not have otherwise been employed. With its very conservative design, the new Capitol became a reality in 1934.

Since statehood in November 1889, Bismarck has become known as the business, cultural, medical, and financial center for central and western North Dakota. Much of Bismarck's economy is still agriculturally based, although less so than it once was. Government and other business activity now make up a much larger piece of the economic pie.

This aerial view of Bismarck, c. 1950s, shows several distinctive landmarks, including the Cathedral of the Holy Spirit (the tall, white spire in the middle of the photo) and the Capitol building (upper left corner). It is a good example of how much the city had spread out from the 1870s. (SHSND 338–3)

One

BECOMING THE SEAT OF STATE & COUNTY GOVERNMENT

CITY GOVERNMENT

This building was Bismarck's city and fire hall for a number of years. Located on the east side of 4th Street between Meigs (now Broadway) and Thayer Avenues, it was replaced by a building at 609 Thayer Avenue. The photo was taken c. 1909–1912. (SHSND A3425)

This photo shows the current City/County Building at the southeast corner of 5th Street and Thayer Avenue. Constructed in 1926, it once was home to the Quain and Ramstad Clinic, Bismarck's first medical clinic. (Langemo 001)

The World War Memorial building, constructed in 1929–30, once was the site for local high school and state tournament basketball games and the National Guard armory. Now used for citywide recreational programs, it offers several gymnasiums, exercise facilities, shooting and archery ranges, racquetball courts, and many other recreational opportunities. (Langemo 039)

After three city elections, voters approved the Bismarck Civic Center on June 26, 1967. The city purchased some land, and the Wachter family donated three additional blocks for parking lots. Located on 5th Streets and Bowen Avenue, the facility attracts many conventions, tournaments, rodeos, and concerts. After the first Class A basketball tourney held there in 1970, it has been a popular venue for many events. (Langemo 002)

COUNTY GOVERNMENT

This photo shows one of the Burleigh County courthouses. The first one was built in 1873 and located southeast of the present courthouse block. A frame courthouse and log jail were built in 1880, when a new brick courthouse was started. The first Burleigh County District Court opened on June 18, 1874, lasting four days with Judge Barnes presiding. (SHSND 151–37)

The present Burleigh County Courthouse, on the north side of Thayer Avenue between 5th and 6th Streets, was approved in May 1929 and dedicated in 1931. Another building, on the south side of Broadway Avenue between Washington and Mandan Streets, was used for about four years and was demolished in the 1960s. (Langemo 003)

The County Detention Center, added onto the county courthouse in recent years, houses the Burleigh County jail and the County Sheriff's Department. (Langemo 004)

STATE GOVERNMENT

A huge parade was held on July 4, 1889, on Main Avenue to celebrate the opening of the state's constitutional convention. Parade participants included U.S. Army troops from Fort Yates, with Major Fechet commanding, various bands, and others. This David Barry photo was taken looking west on Main Avenue. (SHSND A2981)

This photo depicts a joint session of the North Dakota Legislature (date unknown and people unidentified). The first North Dakota Legislative Assembly convened on November 18, 1889, and adjourned on March 18, 1890. John Miller was the state's first governor, and Burleigh County was represented by Senator C.B. Little and Representative E.A. Williams, both from Bismarck. (SHSND C153)

LIBERTY MEMORIAL

ROOSEVELT CABIN

NORTH DAKOTA STATE CAPITOL
1884-1930

© O.J. Gravem, 1931

Copyright 1931 © J. Gravem, Bismarck, N.D.

This O.J. Gravem photo shows the Capitol grounds in the late 1920s, including the old Capitol building, built in 1883 and added onto in 1893 and 1903, and the Liberty Memorial Building, completed in 1922. It also shows the Theodore Roosevelt cabin, now located in Medora, and the electrical plant, built in 1904 to serve the trolley and the capitol, on the right-hand side of the photo. (SHSND C936)

This Finney photo shows the burning Capitol on December 28, 1930. The government departments spent the next few years in the Liberty Memorial building and other buildings around Bismarck.

The governor's office was relocated to the second floor of the Federal building on the northeast corner of 3rd Street and Broadway Avenue. The 1931 Legislative Assembly met in the World War Memorial building on 6th Street in downtown Bismarck. One wing of the old Capitol was repaired, and the Insurance and Agriculture Departments had offices there. (SHSND A3516)

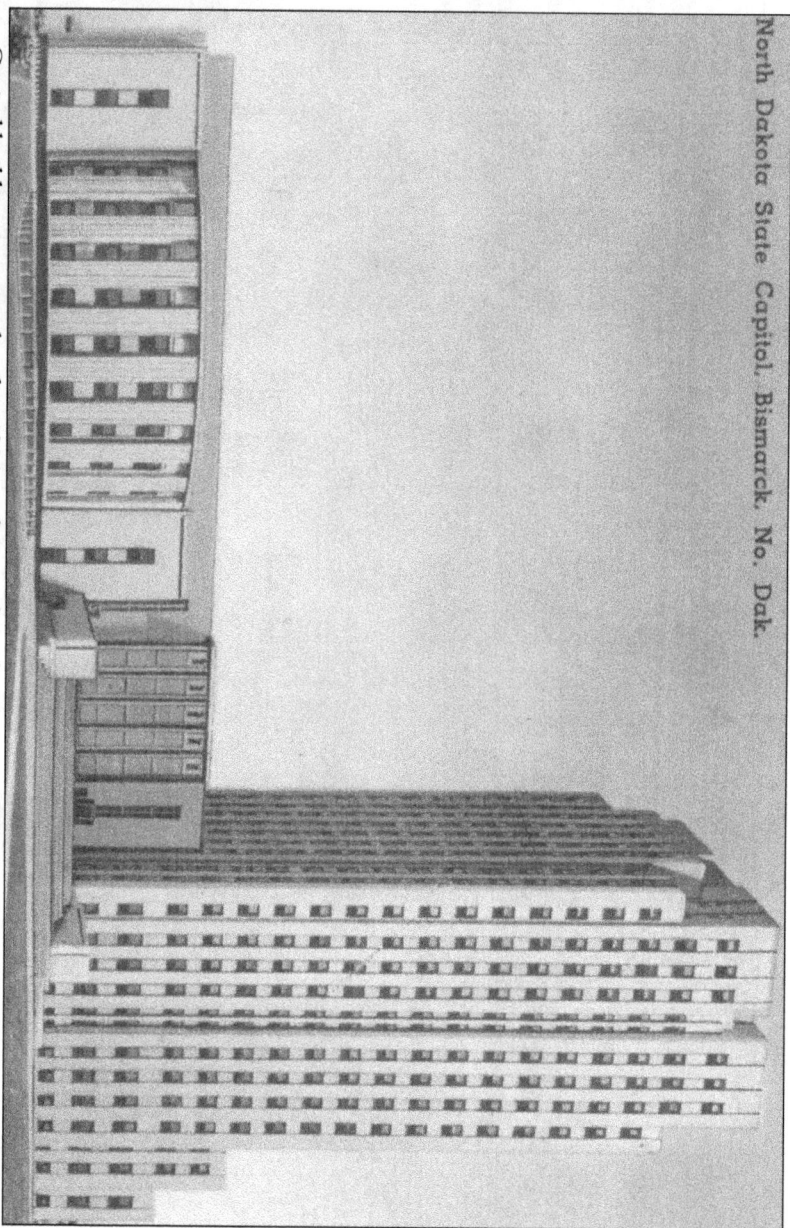

The new, 19-story Capitol building was completed in 1934, and its art deco design emphasized structure over style, with 80 percent usable space. The skyscraper office tower was particularly unusual for the time and contained materials from around the country.

Construction of the new Capitol began on August 2, 1932, with groundbreaking by Gov. George F. Shafer. Located very near the site of the old Capitol, it was planned by architects John A. Holabird and John W. Root of Chicago to be quite conservative, costing just 46 cents per cubic foot. The building clearly shows the separation of governmental functions—the legislative wing, the executive branch in the office tower, and the judicial wing, added in 1981.

The project created jobs for many workers during the Great Depression, and the completion of the new Capitol was topped off with a gala celebration on June 1, 1934. (SHSND B716–38)

16

The Sakakawea statue, a 12-foot high bronze statue erected on the Capitol grounds in 1910, was financed by the North Dakota General Federation of Women's Clubs and sculpted by Leonard Crunelle. A replica of an Indian earth lodge was added on the Capitol grounds just east of the Capitol building in 1930. (SHSND 200–4x5–84)

The Pioneer Family statue on the Capitol grounds was sculpted by Award Fairbanks and commissioned by Harry F. McLean, whose father, John A. McLean, was Bismarck's first mayor. It was dedicated on September 20, 1947. (SHSND 106–73)

This photo shows a meeting in the House chambers during the 1963 Legislative session. In 1970 and 1972, a new state constitution was debated here, as well as in the Senate chambers. The new document was approved by the voters in November 1972. (SHSND C1685)

Other features on the Capitol grounds include the petrified logs and stumps, the horse sculpture by Métis artist Bennett Brien, the buffalo, the John Burke statue, the North Dakota Peace Officers and All Veterans Memorials, the Liberty Memorial building, and the State Heritage Center (middle foreground). (Fowler 001)

A state historic site, the Former Governors' Mansion on 4th Street and Avenue A was originally owned by Asa Fisher. Built in 1884, it was considered a fine house with its running water and steam heat. Eli Shortridge was the first governor to live here, beginning in May 1893, and John Davis was the last, moving to the new governor's residence on 4th Street and Boulevard Avenue in March 1960. (SHSND A2988)

The current governor's mansion at 4th Street and Boulevard Avenue was completed in early 1960. It cost $201,500, just slightly over the budget allocated by the 1955 Legislature. (Langemo 005)

19

Federal land was appropriated in 1881 for a territorial prison to be built in Bismarck, northern Dakota Territory. Opened in 1885, it is located on the north side of the NPRR line about two miles from downtown Bismarck, and other buildings were added over the years. The facility offers assorted work, academic and vocational education, and treatment programs to assist in rehabilitating inmates.

A number of executions have taken place at the Penitentiary, including that of James W. Cole in March 1899, Ira O. Jenkins in September 1900, and John Rooney in October 1905. (SHSND B716–15)

FEDERAL GOVERNMENT

By 1908, the U.S. Weather Bureau was housed at Camp Hancock, on the corner of 1st Street and Main Avenue, with O.W. Roberts as director. The camp was established in 1872 and served as a warehouse and supply depot.

First called Camp Greeley for Horace Greeley, the famous journalist, it was the home of Company D, 17th Infantry, commanded by Captain Clarkey. Capt. B.F. "Frank" Slaughter was the post physician/surgeon. (SHSND B716–20)

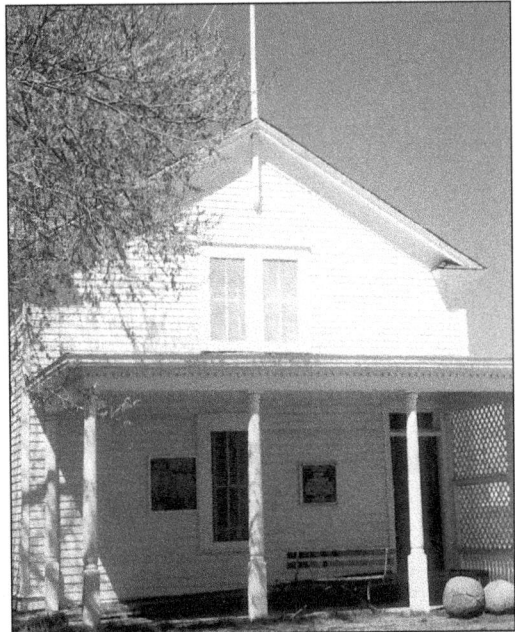

Camp Hancock is now a state historic site and includes one of the original buildings, as well as a train locomotive and the original St. George's Episcopal Church, moved there from the corner of 3rd Street and Thayer Avenue in the 1960s. (Langemo 006)

Completed in January 1913, the Federal Building at 3rd Street and Broadway Avenue housed the U.S. Post Office and other Federal government entities. Before that, the post office was on Main Avenue between 2nd and 3rd Streets, with Colonel Lounsberry as postmaster, and at 315 Main Avenue.

The Post Office has since moved to the new Federal Building on 3rd Street and Rosser Avenue, and the old Federal Building has been remodeled to make additional office space. There is also a major distribution center on Bismarck Expressway and branches at several locations around the city. (SHSND D246)

Here is the old Federal building as it looks in 2002. It continues to be used by several Federal agencies. (Langemo 007)

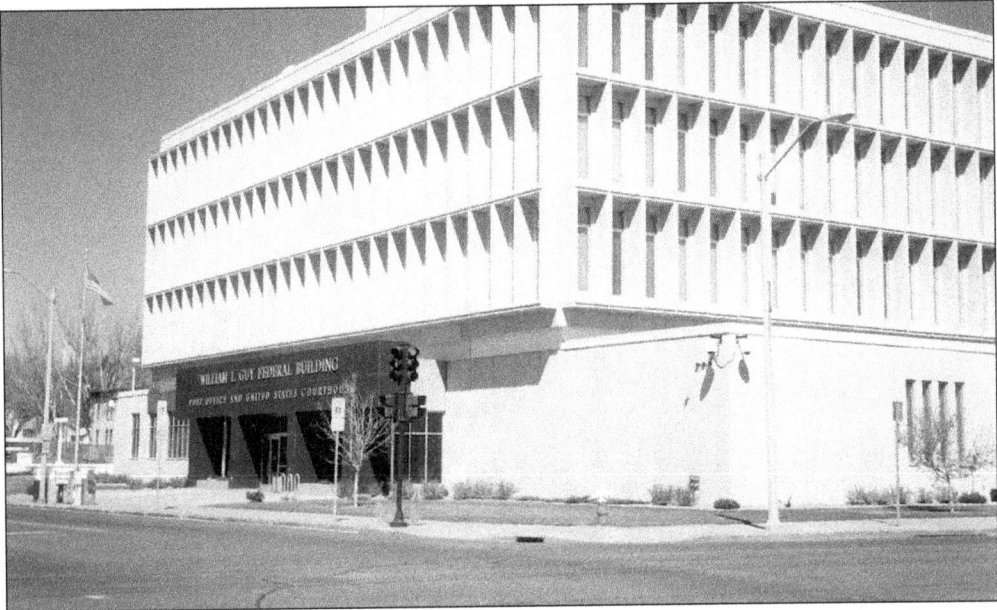

The William L. Guy Federal Building was dedicated in September 1964 and has almost as much office space as North Dakota's Capitol Building. It houses the U.S. Post Office, the offices of North Dakota's Congressional delegation, the Federal court, and many other Federal government departments. (Langemo 008)

MILITARY

North Dakota's National Guard troops left for the Philippines and the Spanish-American War in 1898. As an adopted son of North Dakota, Theodore Roosevelt perhaps generated some enthusiasm among North Dakotans for the war and for his Roughriders. (SHSND C759)

ARMORY CO. "A" N. D. N. G. BISMARCK, N. D.

Company A of the Bismarck National Guard unit was originally housed in this armory on the southeast corner of 2nd Street and Broadway Avenue. Dedicated in December 1908 with a grand military ball, the armory also offered Bismarck a new basketball court. The first game was played on February 21, 1909, between the Fort Lincoln and the North Dakota Agricultural College (now North Dakota State University) teams. (SHSND 339–15)

From the 2nd Street and Broadway Avenue armory, the Bismarck National Guard units moved to various locations over the years, including the World War Memorial Building on 6th Street, the Bismarck State College armory, and now the Raymond J. Bohn Armory east of Bismarck. (NDANG 001)

This photo shows a group of Burleigh County draftees heading off to war on April 29, 1918. Though North Dakota supported isolationism, its citizens stepped forward to do their part once the U.S. joined World War I on April 6, 1917. Bismarck's first casualty of World War I was Pvt. Lloyd W. Spetz, for whom the American Legion Post No. 1 is named. He was killed in action on March 1, 1918. (SHSND A1360)

Fort Lincoln, established as a military reservation in 1895, was developed on 900 acres 3 miles south of Bismarck in 1903. The brick buildings, of modified colonial style, were occupied until 1913, when the garrison was removed. The fort was used again during World War I as a concentration camp and then closed until 1927 when 4 companies of the 3rd Battalion, 4th Infantry, were assigned there.

Fort Lincoln was again used in the 1930s, this time as a Civilian Military Training Corps site. (SHSND A4879)

Fort Lincoln was active through World War II, when it was used as an internment camp for Japanese and German prisoners. The Army Corps of Engineers headquartered at Fort Lincoln during the Garrison Dam construction, and it was a Job Corps Conservation Center site from 1966–1968. Since then, it has been occupied by the United Tribes Technical College, a job training and placement center for Native Americans. (SHSND 996–3)

Featrice Nygaard was one of many Bismarckers who helped sell war bonds during World War II. Two other women, both unidentified, join her in this c. 1940s photo. (SHSND 276–30)

Two

GROWING THE
COMMUNITY
MUNICIPAL, EDUCATIONAL, RELIGIOUS, & MEDICAL SERVICES

Most of Bismarck's municipal services were developed by 1885, including water and electricity. The electrical service was first provided by E.A. Hughes in 1889. In late 1896, the Hughes Electric Company was located at 4th Street and Thayer Avenue, with a power plant on the northeast corner of 3rd Street and Front Avenue. Fire and police protection were other essential municipal services offered by the 1880s.

This 1878 photo shows how water was hauled around town and sold at 25¢ a barrel to Bismarckers. Eber H. Bly was mainly responsible for developing Bismarck's water system. Located on Wagon Wheel Bluff near the Missouri River, two water reservoirs were completed in 1887. After 15 years of water delivery by wagon, Bismarckers had a true water system. By 1919, offices for the Bismarck Water Supply Company, established by Bly, Alexander McKenzie, and R.B. Mellon, were located at 314 Broadway Avenue.

Bly also ran a saw mill, a brickyard, and a coal mine, and he built the Hotel Sheridan where the NPRR Depot now stands.

Bismarck now has a water treatment plant along the river that has been expanded and rebuilt many times to accommodate the city's growing population. (SHSND B363)

This photo, taken on January 1, 1887, is of Bismarck's banner hook and ladder company of the local fire department. The city went to a paid fire department in April 1911, and a new fire hall was built that year for $14,778. (SHSND B313)

The photo, c. 1940s, shows a motorized fire truck that was part of the city's fire department. By 1972, the department had 7 pieces of equipment and 34 firefighters. (SHSND E186)

This photo shows Bismarck's first police force, c. 1890. By 1972, the city had 60 police officers. (SHSND A7254)

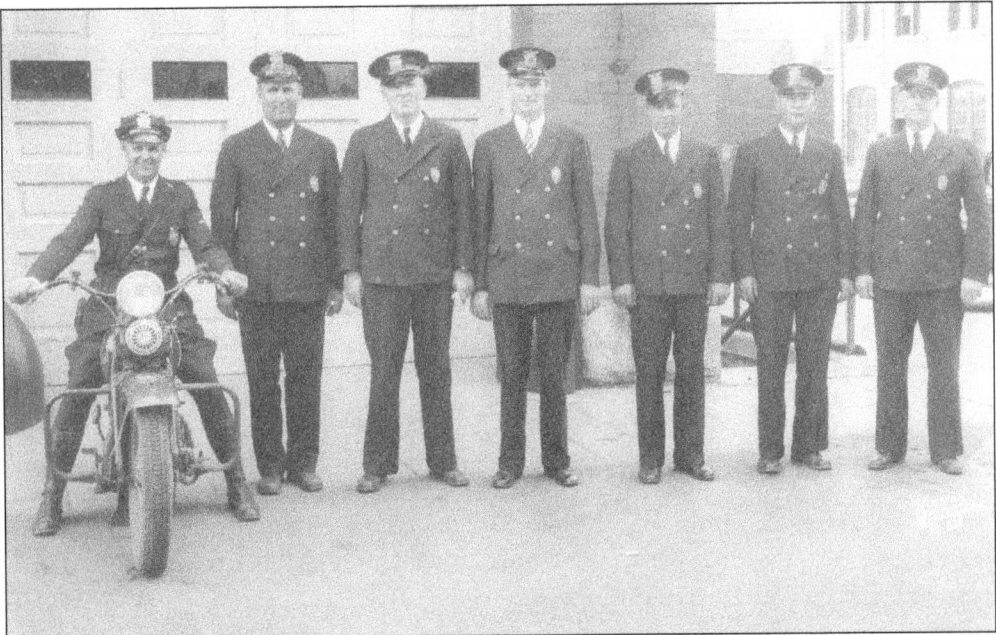

By 1935, the Bismarck police force included several officers and various modes of transportation. The photo includes, from left to right, Charles "Dutch" Graves (on the motorcycle), William Franklin, Joe Shimik, Vince Kavaney, W.R. Ebeling (chief), and Ryder Hamro. (SHSND C920)

The combined city/county law enforcement center on South 9th Street offers one-stop convenience for personnel and the public. (Langemo 009)

This 1935 photo shows Highway Patrol officers including, from left to right, W.J. Flannigan, Frank Patnam, George Swenson, George Robinson, Emil Lundquist, and Curtis Siel. (SHSND D600–2)

This was Bismarck's first high school. The William Moore School, honoring Bismarck's first school superintendent, opened in September 1883 to 364 students. Located at 5th Street and Rosser Avenue, the two-story building cost $4,000. H.O. Saxvik was superintendent, and the school's Demon mascot, meaning "undying fighting spirit," was first used in the fall of 1922.

A new high school building was completed in 1912, and the old high school became the junior high school. The North Ward School, renamed William Moore School, was built in 1884 between Avenues E and F and 4th and 5th Streets. The high school closed in December 1951 after 68 years of use and moved to the current Bismarck High School (BHS) at 723 North 7th Street.

Early elementary schools included Richholt, Roosevelt, Wachter, Will, and William Moore. The Wachter school was torn down in the late 1970s.

By 1961, the city had six parochial schools and a public high school, junior high school, and nine elementary schools. There were six colleges or vocational schools. Just eight years later, there were five parochial schools, along with one public high school, one junior high school, and 12 elementary schools. (SHSND C41)

Actually, Linda Warfel Slaughter established the first school in Bismarck, the Bismarck Academy, in July 1873. A private institution, it was located in the Congregational Church on the southeast corner of 5th Street and Thayer Avenue, and her sister, Aidee Warfel, was the teacher. The Academy moved to the home of Mrs. J.P. Dunn at 208 3rd Street in 1877.

Slaughter was later elected Burleigh County Superintendent of Instruction, the first woman elected to public office in Dakota Territory. She also served as Deputy Superintendent of Public Instruction for the Territory.

The first BHS graduating class was in 1887. This photo, however, shows the BHS graduating class of 1893, including from left to right, Katherine Staley, Fannie Dunn, John Bostrom, Jennie McNider, Maud Robinson, and Pearl Braithwaite.

In 1951, BHS had 148 graduates, while St. Mary's Central High School had 62 and Bismarck Junior College had 66 with 14 one-year certificates. (SHSND D373)

By 1934, the city's only high school was overflowing with its 649 students. A three-story building was completed during the 1935–1936 school year, when C.W. Leifur served as principal.

The school has undergone great change and growth since the 1950s, with continual additions and remodeling projects. The 1986 project involved total gutting, renovating up to code, and adding a vocational education wing. In 1998, the north wing was renovated. (SHSND C939)

34

Century High School, at 1000 Century Avenue, opened in 1976, the year of the U.S. Bicentennial. In that theme, the school's team name is the Patriots. CHS is proud of its championship wrestling and track teams, among others. The school saw an addition and remodeling in the late 1990s. (Langemo 010)

Father Chrysostom Foffa came to Bismarck in September 1876 and started St. Mary's Academy in April 1877; it is located on the north side of Main Avenue between Mandan and Washington Streets. St. Mary's Grade School, between 8th and 9th Streets on Broadway Avenue, was dedicated in February 1908.

Over the years, the Catholic school system eventually added other schools, including Cathedral Grade School and St. Mary's Central High School. (SHSND 25B40)

The Will School, built in 1905, was used for about 50 years in the Bismarck School District. Located on the southwest corner of 5th Street and Rosser Avenue, it was one of the early Bismarck schools. (SHSND A1130)

The Wachter School was no longer used as an elementary school after 1974. Later torn down and now on that site, at the southeast corner of 9th Street and Bowen Avenue, is the Terrace, a housing community for seniors. (SHSND A4322)

This 1950s aerial of Fraine Barracks shows buildings that were part of the Bismarck Indian School, operated as an Indian boarding school from 1907 through 1937. The school had from 50 to 125 students per year and was one of only about 30 non-reservation boarding schools in the U.S.

O. Padget, superintendent for several years, bragged about the great results accomplished at the school. Over 50 percent of the employees were Indian, and many of the students attended local churches. At the end of the 1919 school year, 85 students were enrolled and new buildings were added.

Now the state headquarters for the North Dakota National Guard and the State Adjutant General, Fraine Barracks honors Brigadier General John H. Fraine. (SHSND C1357)

This photo shows a classroom at the Bismarck Indian School. The students learned all the basic subjects, as well as homemaking and occupational skills, such as cooking and sewing.

The girls participated in the Sakakawea Junior Girls Club, and the basketball team was very successful, narrowly missing the championship at the All-Indian Tourney one year, losing the final game 18 to 21. (SHSND D299–22)

Bismarck Junior College started in September 1939 at BHS. With W.J. Swenson as dean, 4 teachers ran classes each day for 73 students. The college moved to 9th Street and Boulevard Avenue in 1955, and to its current location on 100 acres donated by Harold Schafer in 1961. Now Bismarck State College, it has grown from 1 building to 9, as seen in this 1990s photo. (Fowler 002)

Mary College (now the University of Mary) was established in 1947, becoming a junior college in 1955 and a four-year college in 1959. By 1972, the university had 650 students and 50 faculty members. This Steve Fowler photo, taken in 1998, shows the changes in the university over the years, when several buildings and curriculum programs were added. (Fowler 003)

This photo is the Bismarck Hospital School of Nursing 1912 graduating class. Other educational institutions have included Christie's Beauty School, United Tribes Technical College (UTTC), Capital Commercial College and Bismarck Business College.

UTTC, established August 1970, is operated by five Indian tribes and located south of the airport. One location for the Business College was the Lamborn Hotel on 6th Street and Main Avenue. Both hospitals support nursing schools. (SHSND 506–21)

By 1884, the young city already had a library of sorts. The Free Reading Room, on the south side of Main Avenue between 3rd and 4th Streets, offered residents a chance to read and relax.

Bismarck's first public library, however, opened in July 1918 on Thayer Avenue between 5th and 6th Streets and just south of the County Courthouse. A Carnegie library, it served its purpose until the Veterans Memorial Library opened. (SHSND A4305)

Today's Veterans Memorial Library is located on Avenue A between 5th and 6th Streets. It has expanded considerably over the years, now taking up most of the block it is on. As in many other situations, the library is now computerized to meet the needs of its patrons. (Langemo 011)

RELIGION

The Congregational Mission started in June 1873. On 5th Street and Thayer Avenue, it housed Bismarck's first school. It was ruined in an 1877 fire that destroyed Pioneer Drug, John Ostland's livery, Custer Hotel, Yegen's City Bakery, and other businesses.

The First Presbyterian Church started in 1873 in a large tent on Main Avenue. Now 129 years old, it is on Thayer Avenue between 2nd and 3rd Streets.

Started in 1873, the Church of the Immaculate Conception (St. Mary's) was on Main Avenue between Mandan and Washington Streets. The first Catholic church in Bismarck, it was established by Father J.B. Genin. The first mass was Christmas Day 1876 and, by 1908, St. Mary's was relocated to 8th Street and Broadway Avenue. The Catholic Diocese started other churches, including the Cathedral of the Holy Spirit in 1945. (SHSND A1608)

Today's St. Mary's Catholic Church, between 8th and 9th Streets on Broadway Avenue, was dedicated on September 25, 1898. Reverend Chrysostom Foffa was the first resident priest, and the Benedictine sisters served as teachers. St. Mary's served as Bishop Vincent Wehrle's pro-cathedral until the Cathedral of the Holy Spirit was built in 1945. (Langemo 012)

41

This photo shows members of the Second Baptist Church congregation, with the church located on the corner of South 8th Street and Sweet Avenue. It verifies there was a population of African-Americans in Bismarck in the late 1800s/early 1900s. The First Baptist Church was located on the corner of 4th Street and Avenue B. (SHSND 739, Vol. 1, Pg. 14)

Another early church was the Protestant Episcopal Church of the Bread of Life (St. George's Episcopal). Started in May 1873 by Rev. Charles Swift, services were first held at the Capitol Hotel.

Consecrated in 1881, it was on the corner of Mandan Street and Avenue A, then 3rd Street and Thayer Avenue, and then to Camp Hancock and donated to the State of North Dakota for a museum. (Langemo 013)

Trinity Lutheran Church was established at 500 4th Street, at Avenue A. Organized in 1878 and first located on the northwest corner of 7th Street and Avenue C, Trinity was a Scandinavian-based congregation, appreciating the Norwegian services. (SHSND A4323)

Trinity Lutheran Church services were first held in Norwegian at Courthouse Hall and is now located on Avenue A between 3rd and 4th Streets. (Langemo 014)

The Methodist Episcopal Church (now McCabe Methodist) started in 1878 on the northwest corner of 5th Street and Thayer. The building in this photo was dedicated by Bishop Robert McIntyre on April 11, 1909, and replaced the first Methodist Episcopal Church built there in 1882. (SHSND A4300)

McCabe United Methodist Church is now on the southwest corner of 6th Street and Boulevard Avenue just south of the Capitol grounds. The 1969 Bismarck city directory showed 44 churches in a wide range of denominations. (Langemo 015)

St. Alexius Hospital began in 1885 in what had been the Lamborn Hotel on the northeast corner of 6th Street and Main Avenue. It was the first hospital in what is now North Dakota, and was, for many years, the only major medical facility between Minneapolis and the West Coast. Abbot Alexius Edelbrock purchased the 1884, four-story, brick building from Alexander McKenzie and Robert Mellon for $25,000.

Operated by the Benedictine sisters from St. Joseph, Minnesota, St. Alexius started as a 15-bed hospital charging $1 a day for services and became a first-class, 125-bed hospital with 18 physicians by 1915, when it moved to its present location on 9th Street between Broadway and Rosser Avenues.

Sister Boniface (Mary Ann Timmins) came to Bismarck in 1892 and was in charge until her death in 1937. Dr. E.P. Quain joined the St. Alexius staff in 1889, and the first female doctor in North Dakota, Dr. Kate Perkins, practiced there from 1891–1893. Other early doctors and their arrival years include Dr. B.F. (Frank) Slaughter, 1873; Dr. Henry R. Porter, 1873; Dr. William Bentley, 1877; and Dr. S.J. Rogg, 1879. (SHSND B716–13)

The 1915 St. Alexius building has grown into the 749,000-square-foot St. Alexius Medical Center of today. (Langemo 016)

Brought to Bismarck by Dr. Niles O. Ramstad and a $10,000 pledge, Bismarck's German Evangelical Hospital opened in February 1909. A 60-bed, three-story brick building, it also had a nurses' home in the basement. The nurses' home on Avenue A between 6th and 7th Streets was completed and dedicated in June 1917. Expansions made in 1926, 1947, and 1950, considerably increased the patient load potential. (SHSND A2485)

Today's Medcenter One Health Systems includes the facilities in Bismarck, shown in the middle of this photo, as well as several satellite clinics in central North Dakota. (Fowler 004)

This Steve Fowler photo, taken in the 1990s, shows the proximity of the two Bismarck hospitals and the excellent medical community that has developed in Bismarck since St. Alexius in 1885. Medcenter One is shown in the middle of this photo, and St. Alexius is in the middle foreground. (Fowler 005)

This photo shows an early (*c.* 1922) ambulance from Bismarck Hospital. (SHSND 277–53)

Quain and Ramstad (Q&R) Clinic, established in 1900, was first located on the second floor of the Eppinger Building next to First National Bank on Main Avenue. This photo postcard, from 1964, shows the clinic at 5th Street and Thayer Avenue, built in 1926. This building is now the City/County Office Building.

Quain arrived in Bismarck in June 1899. He married Dr. Fannie Dunn, who had graduated from the University of Michigan Medical School. Ramstad came in 1900 and was noted as a very competent surgeon. He married Edna Winchester, daughter of Judge W.H. Winchester. (SHSND A81)

This photo shows the Q&R Clinic staff at its 5th Street and Thayer Avenue quarters in 1927. Sitting from left to right (with year each joined the clinic) are Drs. C.W. Schoregge (1916), F. Griebenow (1909), Niles O. Ramstad (co-founder), E.P. Quain (co-founder), V.J. LaRose (1902), A.M. Brandt (1907), J.O. Arnson (1915). Standing are Mr. Boise and Drs. H.A. Brandes (1919), W.B. Pierce, G.M. Constans (1927), F.P. Frisch, H.C. Anderson, R.H. Waldschmidt (1923), P.W. Freise (1926), and L.W. Larson (1924). (SHSND A5673)

This photo of the Missouri Valley Clinic (now Mid-Dakota Clinic) was taken in 1959. Located at 9th Street and Rosser Avenue, it evolved from the Roan and Strauss Clinic, formed in 1909, and was previously located at 402 1/2 Main Avenue. By the 1980 city directory, it was listed as Mid-Dakota Clinic. (SHSND A2801)

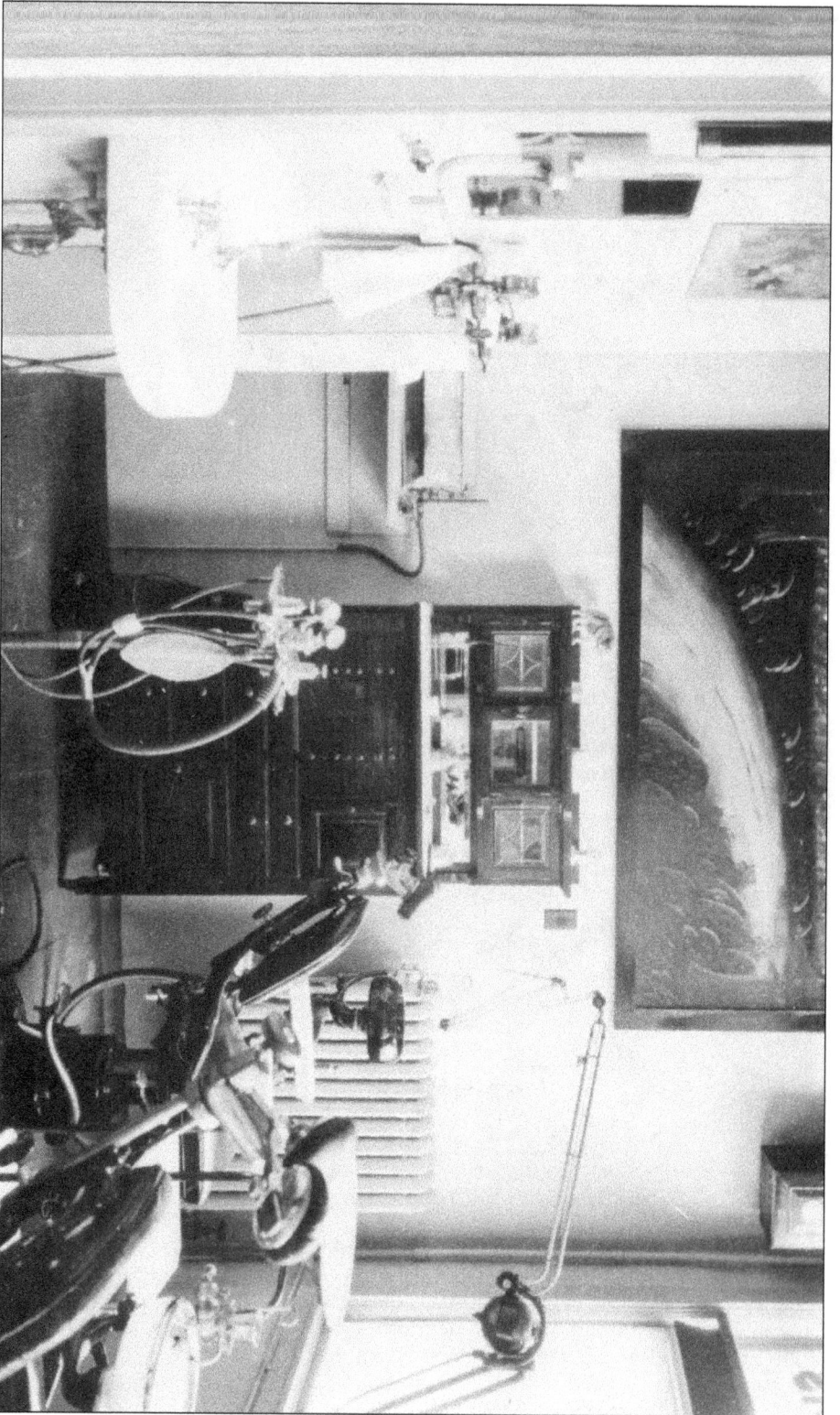

This photo shows the extracting room at the Dr. Charles C. Hibbs Dental office on the corner of 4th Street and Broadway Avenue in the Lucas Block. Taken in 1908, the photo was a gift of Dr. Hibbs to the SHSND photo archives in October 1957. By 1961, the city had 14 dentists. (SHSND A1974)

Three

GETTING AROUND
THE CITY
ADVANCES IN TRANSPORTATION MODES
DEVELOP OVER TIME

Many modes of transportation came together to create the city of Bismarck. The Missouri River brought many people on steamboats and across the river on ferries and other boats.

The railroad definitely caused immigration to pick up. Railroad companies offered special rates to haul families and their goods to the frontier. Obviously, they stood to gain with the sale of railroad lands and through freighting of goods once the land was settled.

Today, the excellent road systems, as well as the airlines, in Bismarck and North Dakota take people to and from the area. Interstate 94, the roadway system across southern North Dakota, was completed in the 1960s, and Bismarck's first commercial air flight arrived in June 1931.

WATER TRANSPORTATION

Steamboat arrivals at the Bismarck steamboat landing averaged 175 per year, most of them for business. However, some were for passenger transportation and even some for just pleasure, like the *Undine*, a Missouri River steamboat, used in August 1885 to carry a Methodist Sunday School group to Fort Abraham Lincoln (Mandan) for a picnic and back. (SHSND A176)

Ferries were often used to carry passengers and goods across the Missouri River between Bismarck and Mandan before the railroad and other roadways were developed to cross. This cable ferry went across the river below Fort Abraham Lincoln. (SHSND 105–8)

I.P. Baker ran a string of boats on the Missouri for many years. The Benton Transportation Company (later renamed the Benton Packet Company) carried passengers and goods to Fort Benton, Montana, and back. This photo shows some of Baker's boats at the Bismarck steamboat landing. (SHSND C253)

This photo shows one of I.P. Baker's boats. His company, the Benton Packet Company, was headquartered in Bismarck, a major navigation center on the Missouri River until about 1885. River traffic decreased considerably as the railroads came through. The last Benton Packet boats ran in 1926. (SHSND A3961)

This photo, c. 1905–1913, is one of the few full length shots of the motor vessel *Bismarck*. Built in 1898 as the *John Bloodgood*, it was renamed in 1900. The *Bismarck* was the first internal combustion-powered boat on the Upper Missouri. The boat burned and sank on June 30, 1913. (SHSND A3961)

The *Far West* became the best known upper river boat. Captained by Grant Marsh, the side wheeler became crucial in transporting the wounded and deceased from the Custer massacre near Hardin, Montana, to Fort Abraham Lincoln in July 1876.

The boat was 190 feet long, had a 32-foot beam, and drew 4 1/2 feet when fully loaded. (SHSND 2821)

RAIL TRANSPORTATION

Before the NPRR bridge, train cars were hauled across the Missouri River on ferry boats. In the winter, tracks were laid, and trains drove across.

The first train arrived in Bismarck on June 5, 1873, shortly before the first *Bismarck Tribune* edition. Thomas Rosser, NPRR chief construction engineer, and Dr. Walter Burleigh, who contracted to grade 50 miles of NPRR roadbed east of Bismarck, are names still in the community. (SHSND C649)

This locomotive, built by Baldwin Locomotive Works in 1904, was specially designed to burn lignite, requiring a larger firebox. It was used on the Bismarck-Washburn-Great Falls line and later sold to the Soo Line. (SHSND B538)

The $1 million, 1,500-foot-long steel bridge (c. 1883) linked the NPRR tracks on the east and west sides of the Missouri River. It was built high enough so that the steamboats could pass under it. However, the coming of the railroads meant a decrease in riverboat business. (SHSND C864)

This *c.* 1910 photo shows the NPRR depot in Bismarck, built in 1901. Located on the south side of Main Avenue between 4th and 5th Streets, it features Spanish-style architecture. (SHSND 339–33)

Bismarck was also on a Soo Line route. The Soo Line depot, a 78-foot-long roundhouse, and a telegraph office, located at 7th Street and Broadway Avenue, were built in August 1902.

Bismarck enjoyed a passenger train until 1979, when Amtrak service ended in Bismarck. Amtrak had announced the end of passenger service to Bismarck in May 1971, but political influence delayed it until 1979.

The North Coast Limited started its run in April 1900, with a run of 69 hours from St. Paul to Seattle. The North Coast Limited was the first electric-lighted train between the Midwest and the Pacific coast. (SHSND 237–9)

56

Fannie Dunn Quain enjoyed bicycle transportation in Bismarck in the early 1900s. (SHSND A3454)

Fannie Dunn Quain also used horses for transportation, riding sidesaddle through the city. Other modes of transportation included the stagecoach. Charles Kupitz ran the Fort Yates/Winona/Bismarck Stage Company line until 1901, hauling groceries, provisions, and passengers.

The Northwestern Stage and Freight Line ran a 48-hour schedule to Deadwood and back. The Bismarck and Pierre State and Express Line was run by William R. Sutley. (SHSND A3454)

In this photo (*c.* 1910), you can see the horse-drawn wagon used by G.M. Mandigo & Son to deliver groceries to customers. The store was located at 210 5th Street. (SHSND 339–13)

ROAD TRANSPORTATION
AUTOMOBILES/TRUCKS

This is one of the first autos in Bismarck, shown near 4th Street and Main Avenue. Francis Jaskowiak built horseless carriages, which created noise on the Bismarck streets. In early 1908, there were only two or three autos in Bismarck.

Some early *Bismarck Tribune* automobile ads announced the Ford Model T, a 4-cylinder, 20-HP touring car for $850 without a top, and a Buick "Flying Devil" runabout priced at $1,000. (SHSND 148–1)

This *c.* 1906 photo shows a Model F Buick, sometimes called the first car west of the Missouri River. It is headed to the ferry to be carried across to the Mandan side of the Missouri River. It is believed to be the first car in Mandan, arriving in 1902. (SHSND 176–151)

The Bismarck and Mandan Ferry, operated over the years by Captain Braithwaite and by Captain Grant Marsh, carried passengers, freight, and vehicles to the Mandan side of the Missouri River and back.

The Rusk Auto House, manufactured by the Fargo Cornice and Ornament Company, Fargo, was the mid-1900s version of a garage. This one was located at 521 North 5th Street and later donated to the SHSND. The photo was used in the *Bismarck Tribune* on May 15, 1973. (SHSND B649)

Long in the dream stage, the vehicular bridge across the Missouri River at Bismarck was authorized by Congress in 1919. Construction on the Liberty Memorial Highway bridge started in mid-1920 and was dedicated in 1922, finally joining Bismarck and Mandan by road.

Part of the Red Trail and the National Parks Highway, the Interstate in North Dakota was completed in the 1960s, and was a major boost to transcontinental travel. (SHSND 422–23)

PUBLIC TRANSIT
STREET/ROAD

The 4th Street trolley line, constructed in 1904, ran from Main Avenue and 4th Street to the Capitol building. The trolley was stored in a barn near the Capitol. The trolley car and an electric plant east of the Capitol were financed through a $20,000 appropriation during the 1903 legislative session. Pictured in the photo are, from left to right, C.J. Herbert, J. Hanson, Lawrence Kasitsky, and Micky O'Connor. (SHSND A3372)

For public transportation, Bismarckers used to enjoy a bus line that ran between Bismarck and Mandan for years. Joseph Dietrich's Old Reliable Omnibus and Transfer Line, with offices at 3rd Street and Thayer Avenue, made stops at the Lewis and Clark Hotel in Mandan and the Capitol Hotel in Bismarck.

The city's bus terminal was at 618 Broadway Avenue, and also provided Greyhound bus service. (SHSND A6843)

This bus driver (c. 1940s) handled the bus route between Bismarck and Mandan. Riders paid 10¢ for a fare or four tokens for 25¢. (SHSND 273–35)

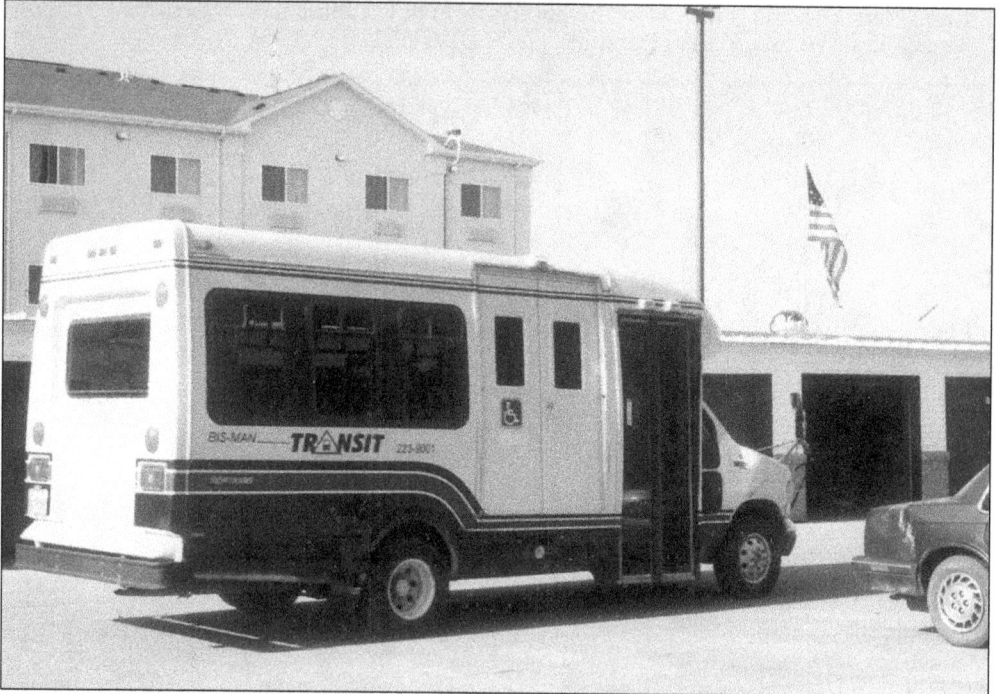

Today, Bis-Man Transit offers transportation to seniors and those with disabilities, while taxi service is available to the general public. The Greyhound bus operates from the new transportation center in east Bismarck. (Langemo 018)

AIR TRANSPORTATION

The Bismarck Airport's first commercial passenger plane arrived in June 1931, although the first airplane flight came in July 1916. Lights were added to the runways in 1934, making the Bismarck Airport one of only two in North Dakota equipped for night flying. More flights were added in the 1940s, and a new airport terminal was completed in March 1966. The airport property grew from 120 leased acres in 1930 to 1,124 acres in 1972, with housing for 70 planes. (SHSND 276–4)

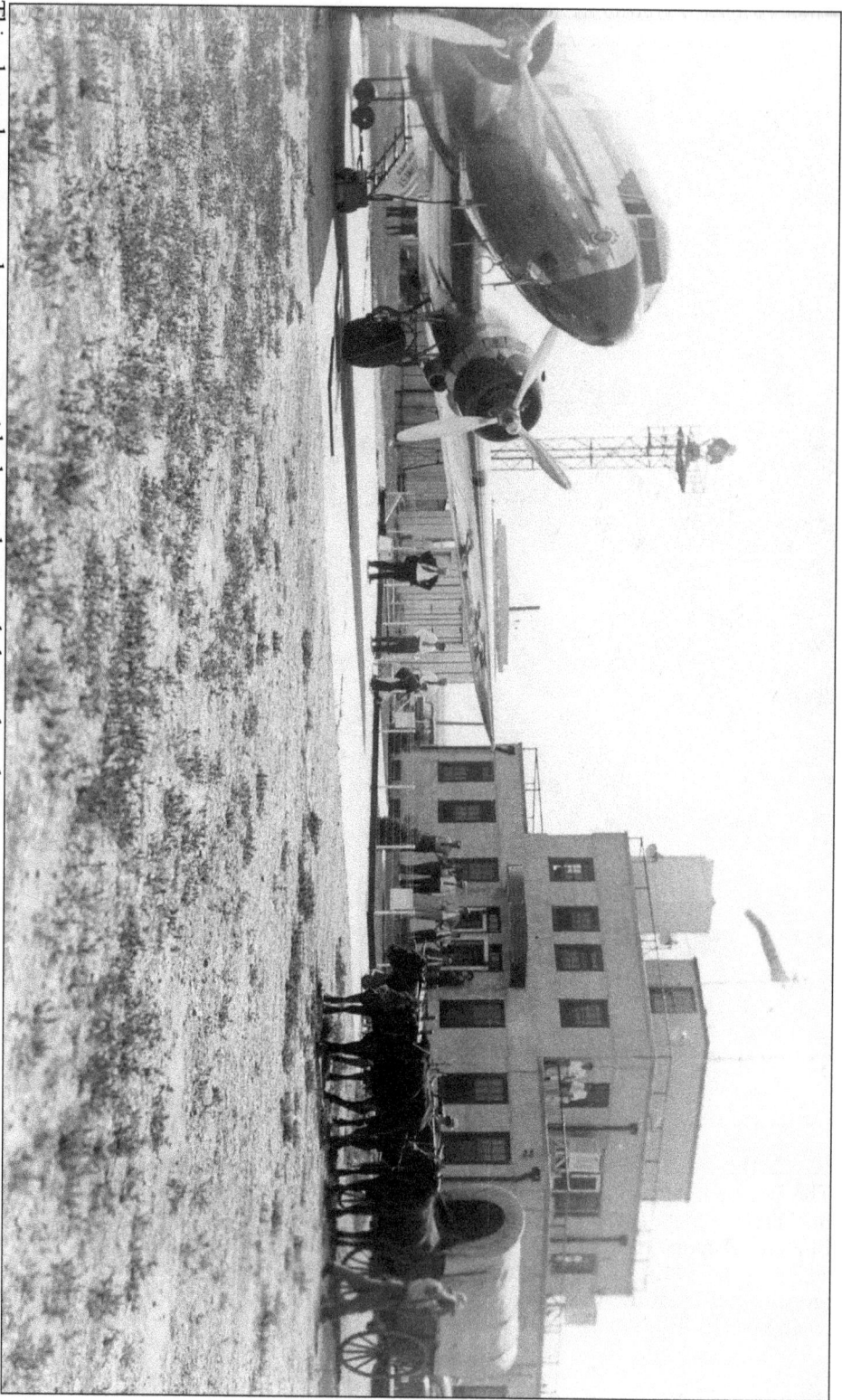

This photo shows tremendous contrast, with the airplane symbolizing the advancements in transportation since the days of the oxen and horse-drawn vehicles. (SHSND A1120)

Four

BRINGING BISMARCK INTO ITS OWN

THE GROWTH OF AGRICULTURE, BUSINESS, & INDUSTRY

Bismarck's business community quickly grew once the railroad came through. By the time the *Bismarck Tribune's* first edition rolled off the presses on July 11, 1873, there were 147 buildings in Bismarck. The fire of 1898 destroyed many of those downtown buildings, but the city quickly rebuilt, mostly with brick buildings.

Sometimes Bismarck was called the "wickedest town in America" because of places like "Bloody 4th Street," the block of 4th Street between Main and Broadway (then Miegs) Avenues. With its saloons, gambling dens, and dance halls came the steamboat roustabouts, soldiers from Fort Abraham Lincoln, railroad workers, and "girls of ill repute." Fights, knifings, and murders seemed to come along with such clientele. By the early 1890s, however, the block was home to many reputable businesses.

The Bismarck Commercial Club was incorporated on January 3, 1906, replacing the Board of Trade established in the 1870s. Located at 119 3rd Street in 1908, it was renamed the Bismarck Association of Commerce in November 1923, it became the Bismarck Chamber of Commerce in June 1954.

AGRICULTURE

This postcard photo, *c.* 1910, shows a Market Day that brought rural residents in to sell their wares and produce and to stock up on supplies. Bismarck's residents still enjoy Farmer's Markets during the summer and fall. Some early farmers included Dennis Hannifin, who arrived in 1873; Dr. H.R. Porter, also with houses in the city; Mike Feller; Henry Suttle; and Alexander McKenzie, with his 640-acre farm. (SHSND 506–2)

George Claridge farmed southeast of Bismarck in Lincoln Township, Section 23. Though the yield was very poor for years because of droughts and other disasters, many like Claridge stuck it out. The 1941 crop was the largest yield since 1928. He was using a 1939 International Harvester Company implement. (SHSND 76–687)

This April 1954 photo, taken by a *Bismarck Tribune* photographer, shows farm workers at the Alex Asbridge farm in Burleigh County. They are, left to right, James McDonald, Emory Woodworth, Leonard Severson, Jacob Severson, Jacob Swenson, Robert Robidou, R.H. LeRoy, and John Yeich. Twelve tractors and other equipment were used to plow and plant the 100 acres of wheat. (SHSND C526)

At the corner of 4th Street and Broadway Avenue (the Hoskins Block), George N. and Richard B. Mellon started the Mellon Brothers Bank in 1882, operating it through 1887. Other banks in the city over the years included the Bismarck Bank, Merchants National Bank, First National Bank, and others. (SHSND A606)

The First National Bank was established in 1879 and was the second oldest bank in North Dakota. This photo, c. 1885, shows the bank on the northwest corner of 4th Street and Main Avenue. The original building burned in August 1898, and another was built on the same site. (SHSND B119)

The Bank of North Dakota, a state institution since 1917, operates on the northeast corner of 7th Street and Main Avenue. It is the only legal depository for all state funds and the central clearing agency for many North Dakota banks and financial institutions. The only state-owned bank in the U.S., a product of the Non-Partisan League, it administers farm, student, small business and municipal bond and loan programs. (Langemo 020)

Wells Fargo joined the Bismarck financial community in about 2000 when Norwest Bank merged with Wells Fargo. One of the largest banking operations in the U.S., Wells Fargo turned 150 years old in March 2002. Founded by Henry Wells and William G. Fargo, the company has been present from coast to coast since 1888. (Langemo 021)

The Hotel Sheridan, built in 1877 along the NPRR tracks between 4th and 5th Streets, was owned by E.H. Bly. It was moved to the southeast corner of 5th Street and Main Avenue in early 1900 to make room for the NPRR depot. Renamed the Northwest Hotel, it became the headquarters for the Non-Partisan League. A day's stay cost $2. (SHSND D482)

The first hotel in Bismarck, the Capitol Hotel was located east of Dr. Burleigh's warehouse, which was on the corner of 3rd Street and Main Avenue. Operated by R.R. and Phoebe Marsh, it was also located at 14 North 4th Street and, when owned by L.N. Griffin, at 62 Main Avenue.

The photo, c. 1875, includes Martin L. (second from the left), a proprietor and relative of Grant Marsh, and J.W. Raymond (second from the right). (SHSND 29–19)

Grand Pacific Hotel, Bismarck, N.

Opened in October 1912, the Grand Pacific Hotel was located on the northeast corner of 4th Street and Broadway Avenue and was operated by Henry Tatley. This postcard photo, with its September 6, 1916, postmark, shows one of the nicer hotels in Bismarck at the time. It started as the Pacific Hotel, operated by Louis Peterson in the same location, and was still in business as late as 1961.

Other hotels included the Custer, Merchants, Metropolitan, Prince, and Soo (Annex) hotels, as well as the Hotel Sheridan (later the Northwest Hotel) and the Hotel McKenzie (later the Patterson Hotel). By 1961, there were 9 hotels and 10 motels in the city.

The Beardsley and Finney Drug Store (later Finney Drug) was located in the Grand Pacific Hotel building, along with other businesses over the years. It was still in business in 1969 at 201 North 4th Street.

The first drug store in Bismarck and in North Dakota, however, was Pioneer Drug. Established by J.P. Dunn, it was located at 92 Main Avenue and later on the northeast corner of 6th Street and Meigs (now Broadway) Avenue. J.P. Dunn had arrived in May 1872 and became mayor in 1884, and his wife, Christina, was a partner in a local millinery shop. (SHSND B716–4)

The Hotel McKenzie (later the Patterson Hotel) was once owned by Alexander McKenzie, a famous and perhaps infamous political figure in Bismarck and North Dakota. Built in 1910 and continuing over a 30-year period, it was located on the northwest corner of 5th Street and Main Avenue. A center of business and political activity, many decisions and deals were made behind the scenes there in North Dakota's early days.

Sold to Edward G. Patterson, who had operated the Northwest Hotel, it remained a hotel until the 1970s when it was remodeled into apartments for seniors and others. The lower level contains Peacock Alley, a popular lounge and restaurant, occupying what was once the hotel lobby and parlor. The Peacock Alley name comes from the decorative scroll work on the outside of the lounge and restaurant entrances.

At seven stories, it was the tallest building in North Dakota when it opened in 1911. The roof garden on the top was the site for many parties and dances. (SHSND E32)

71

The spot where the Holiday Inn now stands has held many other buildings. Just one was the beginnings of the Dan's Supermarket chain (see photo on page 73). Built as the Sheraton in the 1980s, it is the site of many conventions, meetings, and social gatherings. (Langemo 022)

GROCERS & DEPARTMENT STORES

John Yegen arrived in Bismarck in 1872 and set up a tent bakery on Main Avenue. In 1877, he moved Yegen City Bakery to 90 Main Avenue and, by 1908, Yegen Grocery moved to 416 Main Avenue. That building was moved to 810 East Main in 1912 where John's daughter, Margaret, operated it. The store is now at Buckstop Junction, a historic town east of Bismarck. (SHSND A5682)

This is a scene in Gussner's Store, a grocery/butcher/sausage factory on Main Avenue between 3rd and 4th Streets. George Gussner, the owner, moved the sausage factory to 3rd Street and Meigs (now Broadway) Avenue. By 1916, it was at 215–217 Main Avenue.

The people in the photo are, from left to right, George Gussner (owner), Harry Sims, J.P. Dunn, and Frank Reed. (SHSND C474)

When this grocery store was for sale in 1949, Eugene "Bus" and Bert Leary and Roy and Geri Rockstad decided to buy the business. That was the start of what became Dan's Supermarkets Inc., now with four stores in Bismarck. The photo shows Leary and Rockstad's first store on the southwest corner of 7th Street and Broadway Avenue. By 1961, the city had 18 grocers. (Danssmkt 001)

In 1900, the Webb Brothers (William H. Jr. and Philip B.) constructed a building on the southwest corner of 4th Street and Main Avenue, home to the Webb Brothers Department Store, Sears Roebuck and Company, J.C. Penney's, and now Conlin's Furniture. Upstairs were the Federal District courtrooms until the first Federal building was ready. (SHSND A3434)

J.W. Raymond arrived in May 1873 and, before the end of the year, had purchased this building at 47 Main Avenue from E.D. Cummings. He and partner John Whalen stocked clothing and general merchandise. The building had also been occupied by the Glitschka Mercantile, which was later moved to 112–114 4th Street. (SHSND A3283)

74

A.W. Lucas and William O'Hara became partners in 1899. O'Hara left the business, and Drs. C.H. and G.A. Kahler joined. By 1908, the A.W. Lucas Store occupied 116–122 4th Street. Lucas died in 1926, and A.W. and E.O. Mondy bought the building.

This photo, c. 1910, shows the building that now houses Woodmansee's on 4th Street. In 1924, it was the Harris and Woodmansee (William F. and Harry J.) store. (SHSND A3437)

E.L. Faunce operated a general store in the 200 block of 4th Street, selling miscellaneous household items ranging from appliances to paints to hardware. The French and Welch's Hardware Company, a similar general store, was located at 310 Main Avenue in the early 1900s and at 306–308 Main Avenue by 1919. (SHSND C1237)

On the northeast corner of 3rd Street and Main Avenue was the DeGraff's Store (a men's clothing store); it is now is a parking ramp. Built by the Marquis de Mores for a refrigeration house, it was purchased and moved by I.P. Baker to the site in 1898 after the downtown fire. It also once housed a meat packing business, Bakers Hall, and Elbow Room Tavern. (SHSND A3439)

The Montgomery Ward store, once located in downtown Bismarck and later moved to the Kirkwood Plaza Shopping Center, operated until the 1990s. This interior view of the well-known department store shows the best bargains of the day—at least they seem like bargains in today's dollars.

Other department stores in the city over the years have been J.C. Penney's, Woolworth's, and Sears Roebuck. (SHSND C960)

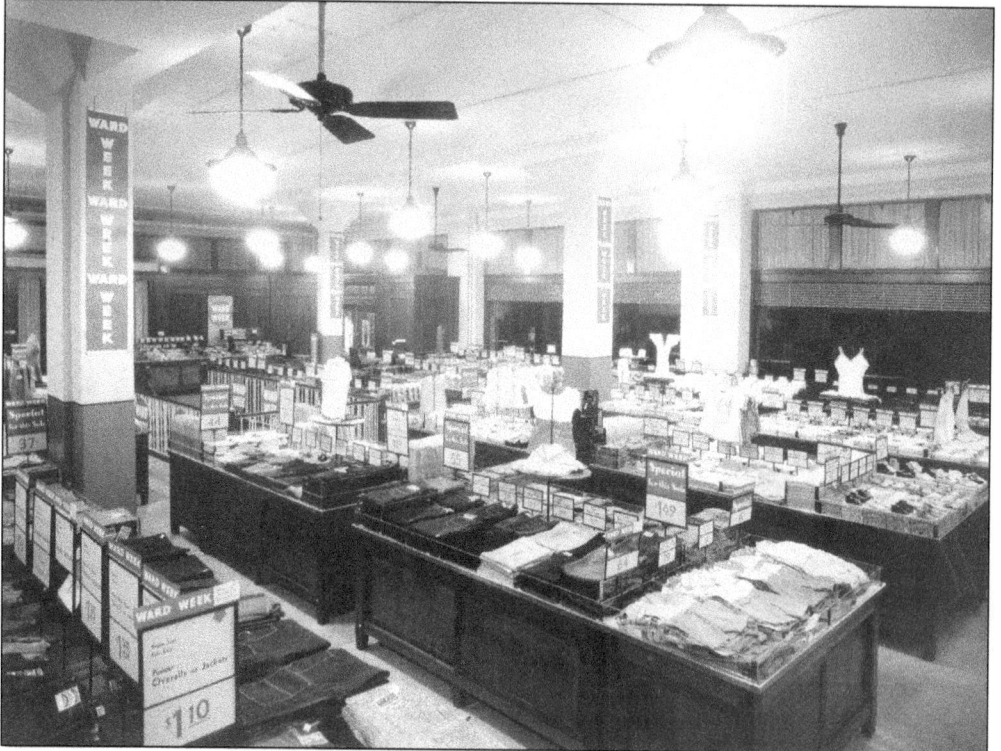

MISCELLANEOUS

G.C. Wachter started the Wachter Dray and Transfer Company on Main Avenue. By 1914, he kept 50–60 teams of horses there. In 1930, Wachter opened a warehouse (pictured here) on 5th Street and Front Avenue. The family once owned most of the land south of Front Avenue, which they donated for the Civic Center, Kirkwood Plaza Shopping Center, schools, and other projects. (Langemo 040)

The Cowan Drug building on the southeast corner of 4th Street and Broadway Avenue was home to J.G. Cowan and family and their drug store/gift shop for many years. The store was first located at 414 Main Avenue. It closed in the 1990s.

Charles Kupitz, along with his wife and son, ran a store and stage line business from the Cowan building. He sold groceries and meat, and dispatched the Fort Yates/Winona/Bismarck stages. (Langemo 023)

The Arrowhead Plaza Shopping Center opened in 1954 on 3rd Street and Boulevard Avenue as Bismarck's first shopping center. Next came Northbrook Shopping Center in 1959 and Kirkwood Plaza in 1970. A 10-year dream of Paul H. Wachter's, Kirkwood Plaza was the largest development in the city up to that time. Opened in 1971, it was expanded in 1980, renovated in 1985, and is currently undergoing a complete refurbishing. (Langemo 024)

Originally the International Harvester building, the Anderson Building was constructed in 1905 on the northwest corner of Mandan Street and Main Avenue. It was later owned by the Anderson family that, at one time, lived upstairs. The building now houses antique shops, a hobby shop, a used children's clothing store and other businesses. (SHSND C1460)

Here is the Anderson Building today. (Langemo 025)

The Capitol Service Station was one of the first gas stations in Bismarck. Located on the corner of 6th Street and Rosser Avenue, O.A. Engebretson's station was one of many that developed in the city as cars became popular. The Medcenter One Health Systems' emergency room entrance is now located where the station once stood. (SHSND C406)

This photo shows a 1936 gathering of a number of Ford Company employees. Carl Tucker and John Fleck are in the front row middle with suits on (and are the only people identified). The company stopped producing the Model T on November 28, 1927, after 15 million were sold. It was an ideal car for its day. By 1927, nearly 161,000 autos were registered in North Dakota. (SHSND C396)

The Barker Baking Company operated starting in the 1920s at 120 3rd Street. Owned by Roy P. Logan and John Hoffman, it was later sold to Warren Whitson and Associates. (SHSND C830)

COMMUNICATIONS

This photo, c. 1875, shows the Western Union Telegraph Company office across the tracks from the NPRR depot. Later, it was on 3rd Street and Main Avenue and was operated by Charles E.V. Draper. In 1908, it was in the basement of the First National Bank building.

Telephone service came in 1881 when C.E.V. Draper constructed the state's first l ong-distance phone line, running from Bismarck to "King John" Satterlund's store in Washburn. In 1884, his office of the Erie Telephone Company was with the Western Union Telegraph Company. (SHSND B242)

The *Bismarck Tribune*, one of the earliest newspapers in North Dakota, began its operation in June 1873, when Col. Clement A. Lounsberry, editor and publisher, arrived with his Taylor cylindrical press. The first edition came out July 11, 1873. The late 1800s saw about eight different newspapers in Bismarck and, in 1908, there were four: the *Bismarck Tribune*, *Palladium*, *North Dakota Herald*, and *Settler*.

The photo (c. 1899) shows the Hoskins Block, with R.D. Hoskins' Capital Bookstore at the front of the building on the northwest corner of 4th Street and Broadway Avenue, and the *Bismarck Tribune*, where Marshall H. Jewell served as editor and manager, taking up the rest of the building. Hoskins' wares included cigars, cards, stationery, books, office supplies, candy, and flowers.

Lounsberry sold the *Bismarck Tribune* to Stanley Huntley in October 1878 and bought it back in 1879. By 1884, it was a daily owned by Marshall H. Jewell. An earlier location for the *Bismarck Tribune* was on the south side of Main Avenue between 2nd and 3rd Streets. (SHSND A3440)

The *Bismarck Tribune* eventually moved its operations to the southwest corner of 4th Street and Thayer Avenue, where it remained for a number of years, until moving to 7th Street and Front Avenue in the 1980s.

The newspaper had only five owners over the years, and only two editors were employed during the 1930s through the 1970s—Kenneth Simons and John Hjelle. (Langemo 026)

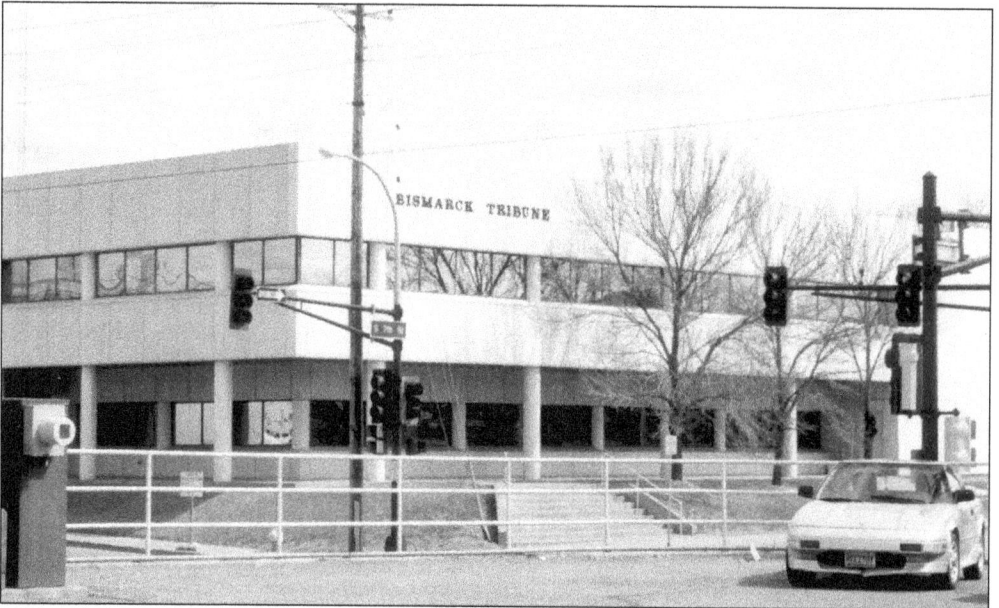

The *Bismarck Tribune* offices and presses are now located on the southeast corner of 7th Street and Front Avenue. It is published daily, with a 100-mile readership area. (Langemo 027)

The license for the KFYR radio station was issued in 1926. This photo postcard shows the KFYR building c. 1927. In 1947, a new $200,000 building at 200 4th Street was planned and, by 1954, KFYR television was also operating. Test broadcasts ran in December 1953, and the first network television broadcasts began in September 1956. By 1962, the city directory showed four radio stations and two television stations. (SHSND A5425)

Other television options for Bismarckers include KXMB TV, with its station at 1811 North 15th Street, and the Prairie Public Television station across the street at 1814. (Langemo 028 and 029)

EATING/DRINKING ESTABLISHMENTS

The Patterson Bar and Grill operated in the Hotel. This photo shows its interesting decor. (SHSND C967)

The Ring, a bar and cafe, was located in downtown Bismarck. The photo (c. 1937–1938) shows the boxing ring at the far end, hence the business' name. Many a boxing match was held at The Ring over the years. (SHSND C423)

Jack Lyon's Hamburger Stand was a popular lunch location. On the 500 block of Boulevard Avenue, the location now contains the University of North Dakota Family Practice Center and the Red Wing Shoe Store. It advertised "the best hamburger in town."

The photograph, c. 1920s, features "Shorty" Klein and Earl Schwartz (manager) in the middle, with Horace Atkinson at the back right and Jeff May, front right. (SHSND A5411)

ASSORTED SERVICES

The Bismarck Steam Laundry Company was operating at 323 4th Street in 1908. In 1928, the Capitol Laundry Company moved into its new building at 309 Front Avenue. The Troy Steam Laundry, operated by Charles H. Albertson, was on the northeast corner of 3rd Street and Meigs (now Broadway) Avenue. (SHSND 336–9)

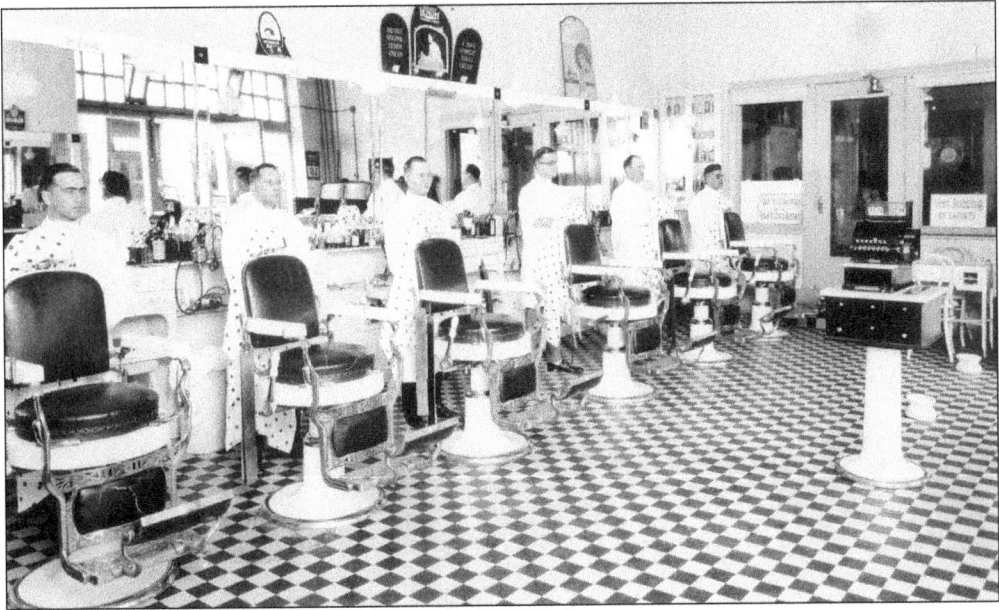

Another business operating in the Patterson Hotel was a barbershop, one of many in the city. This photo shows the six barbers ready and waiting to serve their customers. The Patterson Barbershop was no longer listed in the 1980 city directory (SHSND 70–38)

This photo, c. 1913, shows a lovely wagon from which Emmett Griffin (owner) and his sister, Katherine Griffin Johnson, sold popcorn, peanuts, and other goodies.

Another interesting business was the Okay Confectionary on the northeast corner of 7th Street and Thayer Avenue. Owners Emil and Vi Martin, Freda Zerr, and Martha Kavaney offered Sunday newspapers, penny candy, and pinball machines. It was demolished in the mid-1970s. (SHSND A3203)

Oscar H. Will arrived in 1881 and became a pioneer in vegetable and flower seed adaptation. He used hardy multi-colored corn and other seeds from the Mandan and Arikara Indians to develop a strain suitable for the short North Dakota growing season.

Oscar H. Will and Company shipped products around the world from its warehouse at 322–324 4th Street in Bismarck from 1884 until it closed in 1959. By August 1917 when Oscar died, the company was considered the largest of its kind west of Minneapolis.

The company continued under Oscar's son, George F. Will. Renamed the Pioneer Seed House in 1923, George continued Oscar's mission, producing the North Dakota Corn Show to promote more and better corn varieties.

The SHSND state archives holds in its collections many of the nursery and seed catalogs the company published over the years, beginning in 1885 and ending in 1959. (SHSND C287)

Five

LOOKING AT BISMARCK
ITS STREETS, HOMES, & DISASTERS

Getting the sense of a community happens by getting out and looking over the town. This chapter offers that opportunity–there are assorted street scenes from the downtown area, shots of homes from then and now, and the remains from various weather disasters that have occurred in the area over the decades.

This photo, c. 1910, shows the Bismarck Civic Garden, with the Bismarck Tailoring Company in the background at 118 1/2 5th Street. Charles Kaiser managed the Tailoring Company. To the left in the photo is probably the Northwest Hotel, although it's not identified. (SHSND 339–17)

This street scene, c. 1929, is looking east on Main Avenue between 3rd and 4th Streets. Note the First National Bank in the left foreground, the Patterson Hotel in the left background, and the Webb Brothers building in the right foreground. (SHSND A701)

This photo, c. 1930s, shows several landmarks on Main Avenue between 4th and 5th Streets. (SHSND C953)

Parades like this one, coming up 4th Street from Main Avenue, bring out the community. This *Bismarck Tribune* photo, c. 1953, shows a number of familiar landmarks and businesses in downtown Bismarck. (SHSND C577)

This interesting *Bismarck Tribune* photo, c. 1950s, shows condemned and partially demolished buildings on Broadway Avenue between 5th and 6th Streets. Note the Bismarck Auditorium on the left and St. Mary's Church in the middle background. (SHSND C812)

This photo shows what replaced the condemned buildings in the photo on the previous page—the parking ramp, the University of North Dakota's Family Practice Center, and White Drug. (Langemo 030)

This scene looks west on Main Avenue from 6th Street. In addition to the Patterson Hotel, this February 1973 photo taken by Norman Paulson shows two long-time businesses, Walker's Jewelry and Jensen's Upholstery. (SHSND A5508)

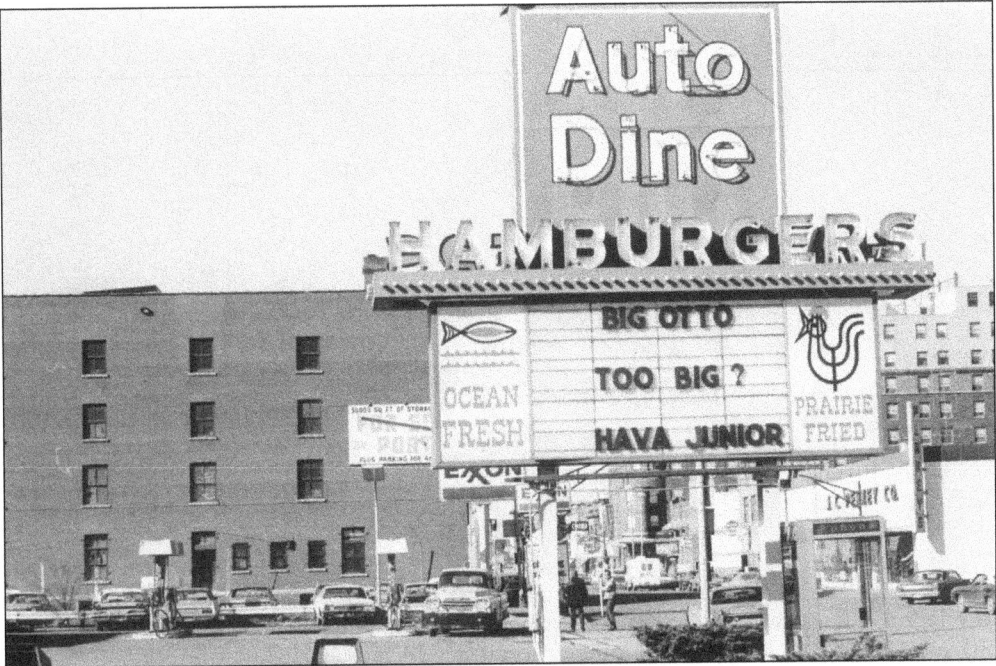

The Auto Dine stood on the southwest corner of 7th Street and Main Avenue where the Rock'n'Roll McDonald's is today. This photo, taken by John Beck in February 1973, also shows the Bismarck Grocery Company building (later the Front Page Tavern) west of the Auto Dine, and the J.C. Penney company on the right. (SHSND A5514)

This aerial of downtown Bismarck was taken in 1998 by Steve Fowler, formerly of Fowler Photography. It shows a number of well-known landmarks. (Fowler 006)

HOMES

The Jackman house was one of the earliest houses in the Bismarck area, built just west of the city near Steamboat Landing and where the Liberty Memorial Highway bridge is now. The house and barn were connected to save going outside in bad weather to care for the livestock.

John J. Jackman led a railroad party to Edwinton in May 1872. Other early settlers were Joseph Dietrich, Mathew O'Brien, and Joseph Miller, Henry Suttle, and William H. Mercer, who were woodchoppers along the Missouri River. (SHSND C837)

This residence belonged to Dr. H.R. Porter and his family. His office was located at 37 Main Avenue. (SHSND 264-36)

This was the home of George D. Mann, *Bismarck Tribune* publisher, and family. Located at 232 Avenue A West, it continues to stand there today. (SHSND C1406)

The James W. Foley home originally stood at 522 North 6th Street. Built in 1907, it was home for the Foley family until 1913, when it was sold to Dr. Victor J. LaRose. In 1972, it became the Elan Art Gallery. The house was moved to Buckstop Junction, the historic town east of Bismarck, in November 1993. (Langemo 032)

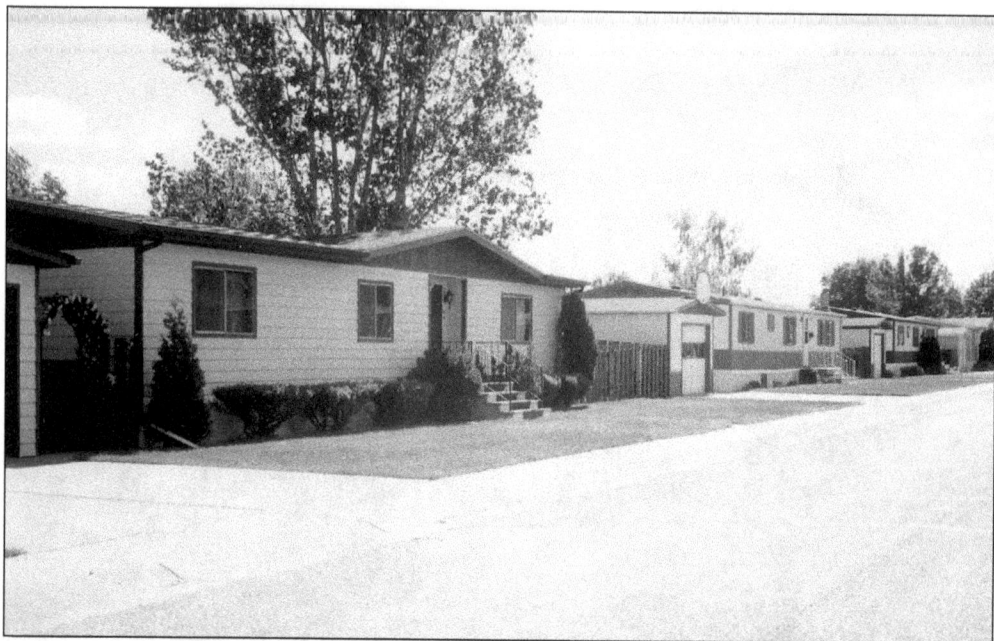

Many middle-income residents have chosen the manufactured home route, as evidenced by Bismarck's 14 trailer courts in 1969. Other popular housing situations since the 1980s have been condos and town homes. And there are the large, luxurious homes in expanding areas, such as Southport, Fox Island, and northwestern Bismarck. (Langemo 033)

With Bismarck's aging population, many retirement housing and nursing home options have been developed in the past 10 to 20 years, covering a wide range of care and cost levels. (Langemo 034)

Much of downtown Bismarck was destroyed by a fast-spreading fire on August 8, 1898. It started at the NPRR freight depot and was not under control until the next morning.

Other memorable fires in Bismarck include the 1877 one which destroyed several businesses downtown; the 1920 fire; and the fire that destroyed the Capitol Building on December 28, 1930. (SHSND 272–2)

The debris on the east side of 5th Street and north of Main Avenue came from the 8th floor of the Patterson Hotel during a severe wind storm. The winds reached 72 miles per hour in the early morning of June 30, 1927. (SHSND A1854)

Floods were not uncommon in Bismarck prior to 1953, when the Garrison Dam was completed. This photo shows the spread of the Missouri River onto the bottom lands south and west of Bismarck on March 27, 1929. The worst was perhaps the 1881 flood, rising to 31.6 feet and displacing many people who found shelter in the World War Memorial building. (SHSND 200–6x8–458)

The spring 1952 Missouri River flood was the last major flood in the area. On April 6, the river topped its 1881 record by .3 inches, and the water came as far north as Front Avenue. It caused Bismarck residents to look forward to the operation of the Garrison Dam. The next year, President Eisenhower would be in Bismarck to dedicate the dam. (SHSND 276–23)

The March 1966 blizzard was one of the worst ever in North Dakota. Though warnings were issued days ahead of time, many ignored them. Raging for three days, residents were snowed in, vehicles were totally covered, and many houses had drifts up to the roof. (SHSND 56–46)

The historic June 2001 hail storm left residents cleaning up for weeks and still doing repairs on their homes and other buildings a year later. This *Bismarck Tribune* photo shows the hail build up in the underpass on 7th Street between Main and Front Avenues. (Tribune 001)

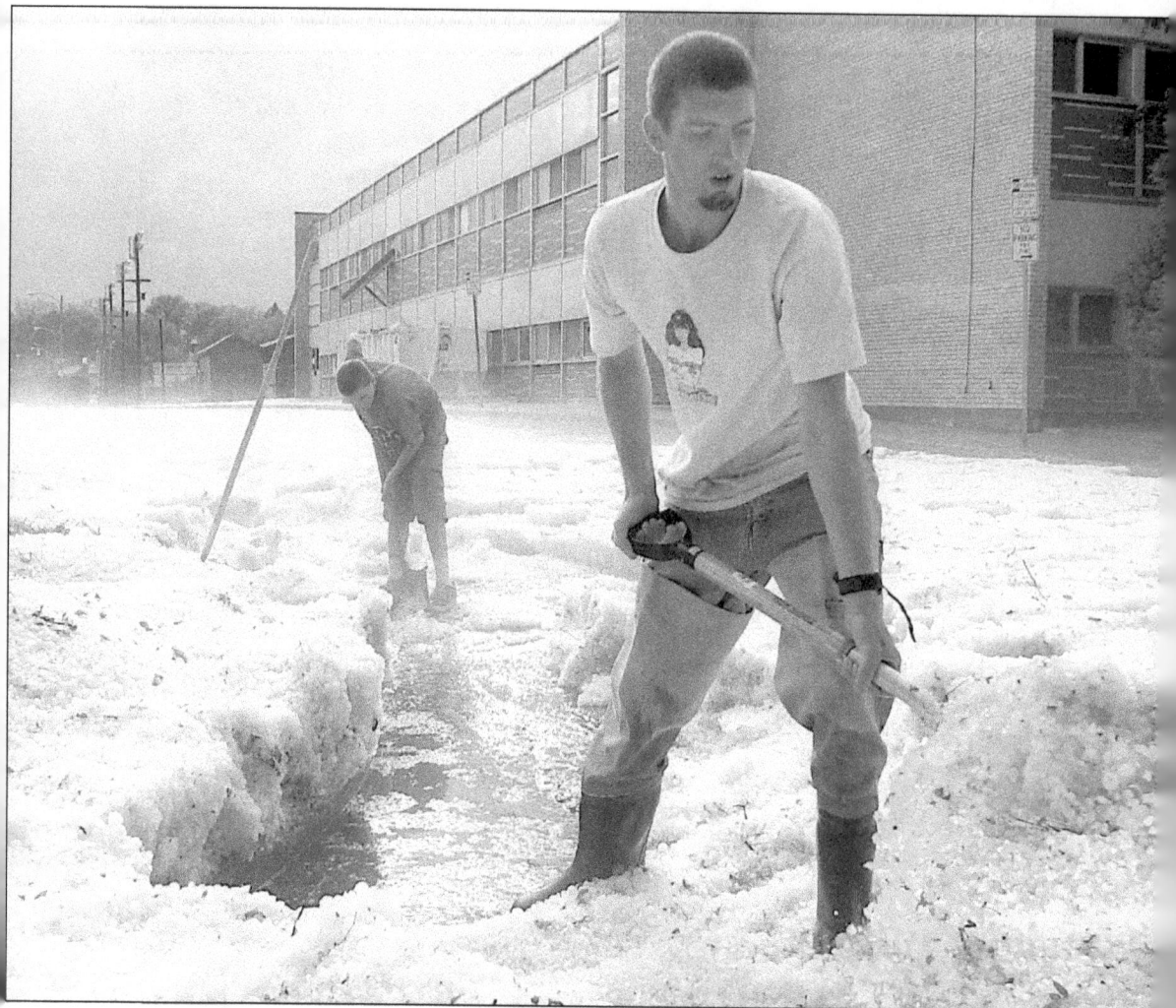

This *Bismarck Tribune* photo shows clean-up efforts at Hughes Middle School on Washington Street and Avenue D after the major hail storm in June 2001. It caused millions of dollars in damage to homes and vehicles. (Tribune 002)

Six

Expanding Minds, Activating Bodies
Music, Art, Culture, &
Recreational Opportunities

Even on the frontier, where people were working so hard to start new lives, there was time for entertainment and fun. There was time for carnivals, parades, concerts, and plays. There was also time for community involvement in organizations and volunteer efforts.

This late 1800s photo shows a carnival on Bismarck's Main Avenue between 4th and 5th Streets. It portrays a great deal of activity, with many people bustling about. (SHSND E748)

Bismarck's Diamond Jubilee was a time for celebration. Those 75 years saw a great many changes in the young city, and the parade was an opportunity to show some of those changes. (SHSND 276–14)

The theater was an outlet in the early 1900s. A favorite entertainment spot was the Grand Theatre at 219 4th Street (c. 1910s).

The Atheneum, a popular spot, also served as a roller skating rink, with S.H. Emerson and Company as proprietor. On the north side of Main Avenue between 6th and 7th Streets, it reopened as the Bijou in May 1907, offering vaudeville, songs, and movies. (SHSND A6778)

The Paramount, in the Eltinge Building on the 200 block of 3rd Street, was one of the early Bismarck theaters. Others included the Atheneum, Bismarck at 204 3rd Street, Capitol (later the Cinema) at 412 Main Avenue, State at 204 6th Avenue, Dakota at 401 4th Street, Orpheum, Gem, and Rex. (SHSND 1075–13)

Though the movies we see today and the technology are much different, the marquees on the outside of theaters haven't changed a whole lot. Here's a shot of the Grand Theatres in north Bismarck with its 10 individual theaters in one location. (Langemo 035)

Music was an important outlet for people on the frontier. This photo shows a band playing on Main Avenue between 4th and 5th Streets, c. 1898. (SHSND A5520)

This photo shows a Bismarck Band concert, with director Thomas Poole. It was held at the Atheneum in 1896. Band members pictured here are as follows: (left row) George Upright, M. O'Connor, Frank Hughes, and unidentified; (center row) William Pattee, William Braithwaite, Thomas Luyben, Albert Marcellus, and unidentified; (center rear) Ben Belk; (right row) J. Philbrick, R.D. Hoskins, unidentified, and Max Kupitz. (SHSND E166)

The Salvation Army band posed for this photo in 1938. Pictured from left to right are as follows: (1st step) Maj. W. Millar; (2nd step) Rozella Sjobom (or Sjoblom) and Bob Radspinner; (3rd step) Bob Gray, Mrs. Millar, and Pete Lepo; (4th step) Connie Arnold, Alice Meader, Janet Millar, Violet Fagerstrom, and Bea Arnold; (5th step) Lt. Arthur Anderson, Leona Sjoblom, Terry Schmidt, and Lt. Hokanson; (6th step) Nellie Anderson, Ray Wirth, George Stebbins, Gust Sjoblom, Leonard Johnson, and Ethel Meader. (SHSND C1418)

This rhythm band was from the 3rd grade of St. Mary's School. It was taken in 1934. (SHSND C433)

This photo shows off the 1941 BHS band, along with its director, Clarion E. Larson. He led the Bismarck High School band for 24 years, and directed the annual community production of Handel's "The Messiah" for 65 years. (SHSND C942)

The Bismarck Auditorium, built in 1913, was the center of cultural activities in the young city. This photo, c. 1910, shows it on the northeast corner of 6th Street and Broadway Avenue before the World War Memorial building was constructed to the north. (SHSND 339–10)

The Bismarck Auditorium was renamed the Belle Mehus Auditorium, after a long-time Bismarck piano teacher. She opened the Mehus Conservatory of Music in January 1966 at 721 E. Rosser after being on the top floor of the Eltinge building for 35 years. (Langemo 036)

Billiard games were just one type of recreation available to residents of the young city. This photo is of the American Billiard Parlor, owned by George and Nick Bittis and operated at 118 North 5th Street. The first billiard hall in Bismarck was operated by Mike Tippie, and another popular one was Pioneer Billiard Hall, opened in 1872 by Asa Fisher. (SHSND 435–127)

The Bismarck Speed-Way Track became a popular place for drivers to sharpen their racing skills and for spectators to cheer on their favorite racers. (SHSND D459)

Children and adults alike enjoyed kitten ball on this diamond on the northwest corner of Washington Street and Boulevard Avenue, just south of where the North Washington softball diamonds are today. (SHSND C770)

Golf was popular in the early 1900s, just as it is today. This photo shows the Bismarck Country Club in 1928, alone on the hill where it still stands. (SHSND 1075–18)

Bismarck residents in the 1950s enjoyed recreation on the Missouri River. This photo, taken in August 1959, shows a Bismarck marina along River Road. (SHSND 907–20)

Two young women, Carol Becker and Sharon Aho, enjoy cross-country skiing in the northeast part of the Capitol grounds in 1954. (SHSND C1307)

Here is Santa Claus water skiing on the Missouri River on December 22, 1957. This *Bismarck Tribune* photo proves how nice the weather can be in Bismarck in December. (SHSND B629)

Many clubs and fraternal and civic groups have been organized in Bismarck over the decades. This photo records a meeting of the Fortnightly Club, the oldest women's study club in the city. Seated from left to right are Mmes. J.E. Davis, John Burke, T.C. Simle, Miss Elizabeth Jones, Mmes. Frederic George Norris, Niles O. Ramstad, and Clyde Young. Standing left to right are Mmes. Florence Davis, E.J. Taylor, Fred Conklin, and Fannie Dunn Quain. (SHSND A1990)

Freemasonry came to Bismarck in 1874, and a charter was granted in January 1876 for Lodge No. 120. In 1880, Bismarck entered the Grand Lodge of Dakota as No. 16. Col. Clement Lounsberry was the first master of lodge. This photo shows an early Masonic Temple, dedicated in February 1912 at 117 3rd Street. Other locations were 3rd Street and Main Avenue and 113 3rd Street. (SHSND 133–10)

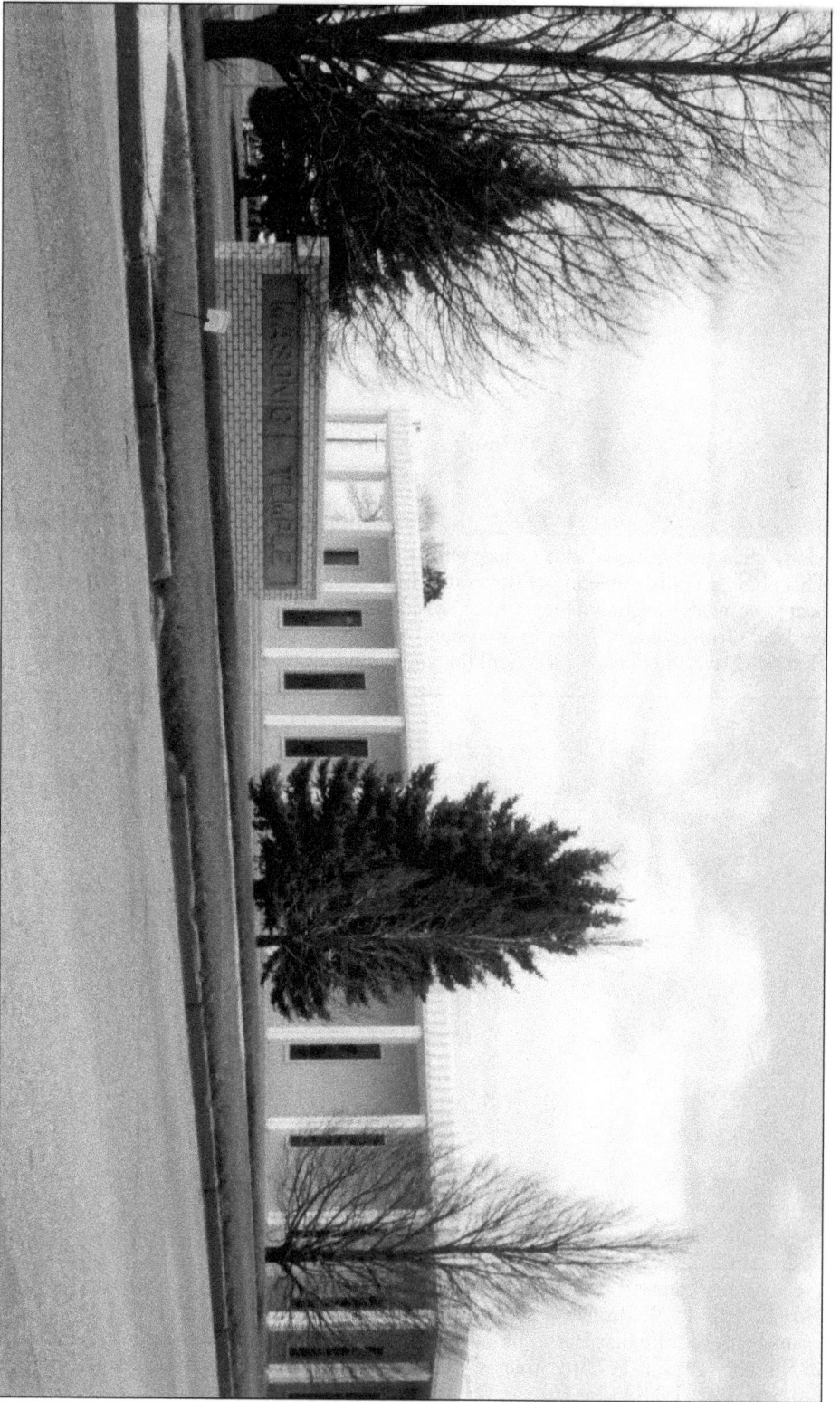

This photo shows the current Masonic temple on Schafer Street near Bismarck State College. It was dedicated on May 20, 1967. (Langemo 037)

112

Many residents of Bismarck have enjoyed volunteer activities over the years. This photo, taken in 1935, shows people involved in the Open Your Heart Campaign. A.E. Thompson headed the 1935 campaign, which delivered 143 baskets of food to needy families in the area. (SHSND D463)

The five-acre Custer Park was the first park in Bismarck. Developed in 1909, it was the project of several Bismarck women headed by Mrs. W.F. Cushing.

Other city parks include Hillside, with land from the Hillside Dairy and St. Mary's cemetery; 60-acre Riverside (now Sertoma) Park, created through CCC work in 1928; Kiwanis, on 10 acres south of the baseball park on South Washington Street; Sibley Island Park, developed in 1937 through WPA work, and General Sibley, dedicated in May 1967, both of which are located on South Washington; the 50-acre Pioneer Park, a joint gift of the Burleigh County Pioneer Association and the Bismarck Hospital Nurses in 1930; and a park on 7th Street and Bowen Avenue donated by O.H. Will and Company.

By 1961, the city had seven parks and, in 1972, the Bismarck Parks and Recreation Board owned 1,200 acres of land. The 1980 city directory showed 30 parks and 1,447 acres. (Langemo 038)

114

Seven

BRINGING BISMARCK TOGETHER

SCHOOL, AMATEUR, SEMI-PRO, & PRO SPORTS & ATHLETICS

Bismarckers have always been excited about sports—strongly supporting school and city sports teams. This chapter is just a small sampling of some of the teams in Bismarck over the years. Many more are available at the SHSND photo archives at the State Heritage Center or by contacting the various schools.

This is a photo of the Bismarck Junior High School basketball team in 1925 after participating in the Knowles basketball tournament. In the front row, holding the ball, is Lawrence Kositzky. The middle row includes, from left to right, John O'Hare, Fay Brown, Ben Jacobson, Harry Scroggins, unidentified, and Dick Register. In the back row, from left to right, are Marie Huber, Earl Hoffman, and the coach. (SHSND C377)

This 1932 St. Mary's basketball team photo includes Rev. Father Hollaman (back row on the left) and Coach Arnold Van Wyk (back row on the right). Team members are not identified. (SHSND C1720)

The 1935 BHS basketball team includes, in the front row, from left to right, unidentified, Neil Croonquist, William Owens, Lewis Beal, and unidentified. In the back row, from left to right, are Coach McLeod, Oliver Sorsdahl, Bud Kanz, Leon Doerner, Bob Peterson, and James McGinnis. (SHSND C380)

The Bismarck Indian School featured many championship athletic teams including this 1935 basketball team, with Bryce Doyle as coach. Team members are not identified. (SHSND D299–16)

Hockey has been a popular sport in Bismarck for many years. This photo features the 1935 BHS hockey team. In the front row, from left to right, are Pinky Register, Curtis Wedge, Wilson Davis, Jock Smith, Paul Raduns and Lucius Wedge. In the back row, from left to right, are Coach Joe Meyers, George Paul, Charles Jordan, Orville Monral, Roland Swirck, and Coach George Schaumberg. (SHSND C1717)

118

The 1935 BHS girls' tumbling team shows off one of its routines. Team members are not identified. (SHSND C1294)

This 1937 BHS basketball team shows the Demons mascot name on the jerseys. Included on the team, in the front row, from left to right, are Harold Smith, Robert Welch, Warren Kraft, Charles Connor, Harry Rishworth, Harold Spangler, and Bob Burkhardt. In the back row, from left to right, are Coach Glenn Hanna, Alvin Potter, Lewis Beal, Gilbert Olson, Bob Peterson, Bob Tavis, Glenn Enge, and Jack Bowen. (SHSND C941)

This photo, date unknown, features the BHS baseball team. The bottom row, from left to right, includes unidentified, Frank Goetz, Bud Beall, unidentified, and Alfred Ellofson. In the middle row, from left to right, are Jim Burkhardt, Ronald Erickson, Urbin Hagen, unidentified, and Jim McGinnis. The top row includes, from left to right, Coach T. Simle, Giggs Boelter, ? Stratton, Chris Baker Sr., two unidentified players, and Coach Myron Anderson. (SHSND C381)

This 1889 photo features the Bismarck city baseball team. John Homan is standing second from the right. Umpire William A. "Billy" Falconer is in the center. (SHSND 435–6)

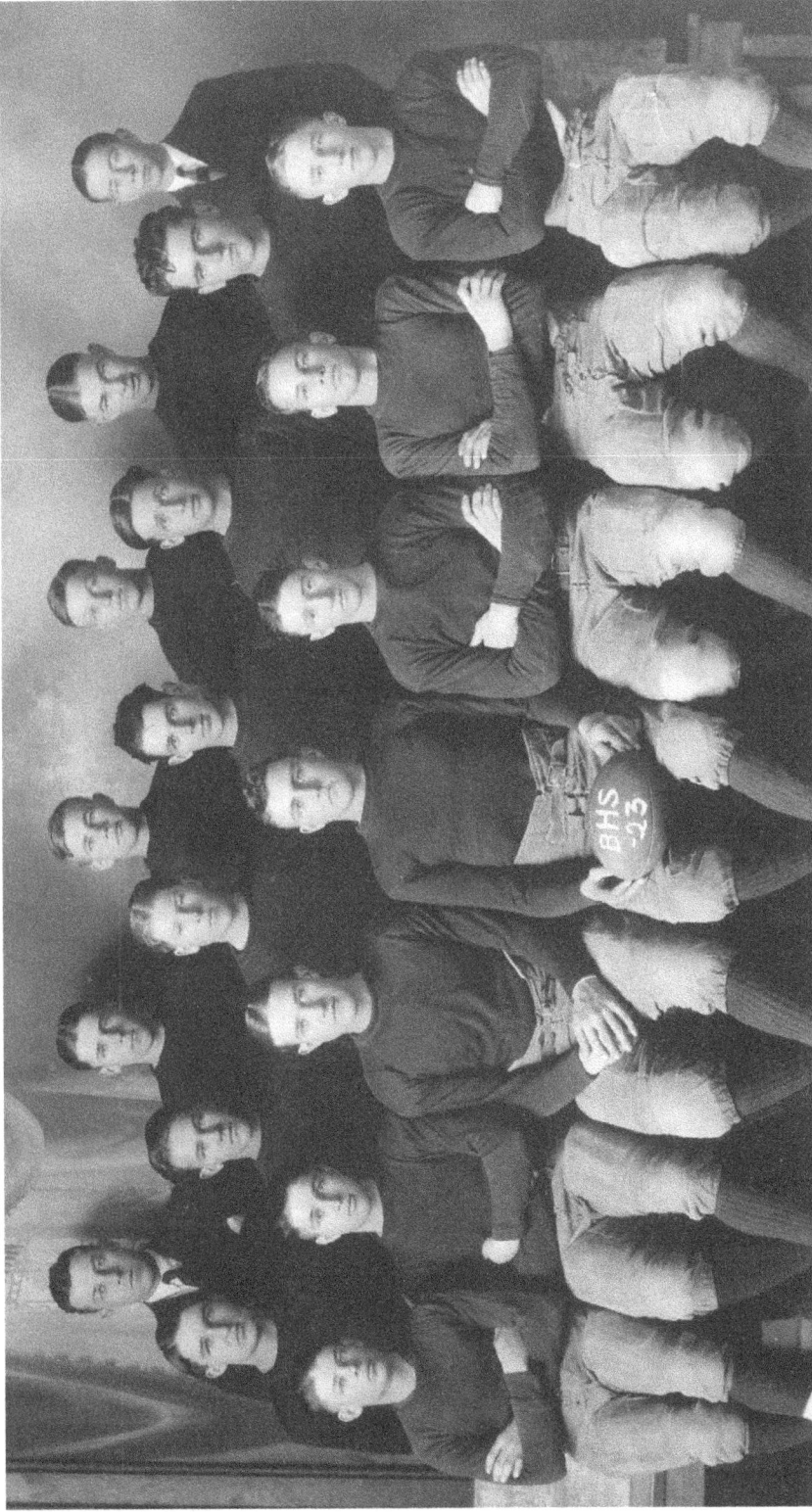

The 1937 Bismarck Phantoms basketball team made its way to the State Independent Basketball Championships. This team was supported and recruited by Bismarck businessman Neil Churchill.

Churchill also supported and recruited players to the 1930 national championship Bismarck baseball team, starring Satchel Paige and other players who had successful baseball careers. Paige went on to success in the Negro Leagues, in a time before baseball was integrated by Jackie Robinson. (SHSND C378)

This photo, c. 1925, shows the Grove (State Penitentiary) All-star baseball team. Team members are not identified. (SHSND D344-A)

INDEX

127

BIBLIOGRAPHY

Assorted magazine and newspaper articles, flyers, brochures, etc.

Bauman, Beth Hughes, and Dorothy J. Jackman. *Prairie Trails to Hi-Ways*. 1978.

Biek, Robert F. *A Visitor's Guide to the North Dakota Capitol Grounds*. 1995.

Bird, George F., and Edwin J. Taylor Jr. *History of The City of Bismarck, North Dakota—The First 100 Years—1872–1972*. 1972.

Blackstead, David J., executive editor. *Bismarck 100—1872–1972*. 1972.

Heindenreich, Virginia L . *North Dakota's Former Governor's Mansion: Its History and Preservation*. 1991.

Naylor, Cliff, and Ken Wosepka (CK Productions). *The 125th Anniversary Video of Bismarck*. 1997.

Polk. Assorted Bismarck City Directories.

Remele, Larry. *The North Dakota State Capitol: Architecture and History*. 1989.

Skyscraper Capitol (video).

www.ingramcontent.com/pod-product-compliance
Lightning Source LLC
Chambersburg PA
CBHW080559110426
42813CB00006B/1352